Also by Ethel Pochocki

Once Upon a Time Saints

More Once Upon a Time Saints

One-of-a-Kind Friends: Saints and Heroes for Kids

The Wind Harp and Other Angel Stories

The Fox Who Found Christmas

Grandma Bagley to the Rescue

A Penny for a Hundred

The Attic Mice

around the year Once upon a time saints

ethel Pochocki
with illustrations By Ben hatke

BETHLEHEM BOOKS · IGNATIUS PRESS

BATHGATE, ND   SAN FRANCISCO

Nihil Obstat:
  Rev. Hilarion Kistner, O.F.M.
  Rev. John J. Jennings

Imprimi Potest:
  Rev. Jeremy Harrington, O.F.M.
  Provincial

Imprimatur:
  +Daniel E. Pilarczyk, V.G.
  Archdiocese of Cincinnati
  July 31, 1979; January 10, 1980
  May 22, 1980; July 14, 1981

First Bethlehem Books Printing April 2009

ISBN: 978-1-932350-26-5.
Library of Congress Control Number: 2008943664.

Bethlehem Books
10194 Garfield Street South
Bathgate, North Dakota 58216
www.bethlehembooks.com
1-800-757-6831

Printed in the United States of America on acid-free paper

Manufactured by Thomson-Shore, Dexter, MI (USA); RMA120JM99, June 2016

Contents

Foreword

This third collection of *Once Upon a Time Saints* stories, bursting with saintly—not to mention angelic—deeds and happenings, shows afresh that once Our Lord opened the door between heaven and earth, anything may happen—and does! The saints, having slipped into their heavenly places, have also found ways to slip back in the other direction: with their prayers and their help; sometimes ending up with their very own niche on our earthly calendar.

These "saints days," given to us by the Church, help us to remember the altogether real people who once dwelt upon this earth and who now cheer us on from their heavenly home. Listening to their stories is like hearing their voices calling out to us, saying, "Look what God can do!" From Doubting Thomas to ever-interrupted Frances of Rome to gift-giving St. Nicholas, the adventures of their day-to-day lives (exhilarating or wearisome) encourage, challenge and comfort us. They gently, and sometimes more insistently, remind the world again and again how time and eternity come together in Christ Jesus.

Beginning in the dark of December, the start of the Church Year, this book contains stories and poems for each month. Each tale or verse—whether of heavenly apparitions in a tiny Irish village or of friars who float in the air or of entire countries single-handedly converted to Christianity—makes quite plain that heaven doesn't keep to its place at all, but is happily determined to spill over into earthly life—here, there and . . . all around the year.

– Bethlehem Books

*F*OR PARENTS, GRANDPARENTS, GODPARENTS,
SISTERS, BROTHERS, UNCLES, OR AUNTS
WHO FOR SOME REASON
FIND THIS BOOK IN YOUR HANDS

What was said in preface to *Once Upon a Time Saints* (and again in *More Once Upon a Time Saints*) may be repeated here: these stories were written to disarm rather than alarm. They are meant to show that the saints were not marshmallows—pale, sticky-sweet glops of goo that could be interesting only when toasted. They are meant to show human and lovable (most of the time) people whose passion for God led them into preposterous escapades.

Their lives are as unbelievable, as fantastic, as fairy tales of princesses with golden hair, princes on white stallions, blacker-than-hell witches, elves, pookahs, black ravens, white rabbits and smoke-belching dragons.

Fairy tales clear the way for sanctity. They are the child's first morality play, clear-cut, no-nonsense black and white, good and evil, life and death—with a bit of fun thrown in to alleviate the pain. The lives of the saints, so filled with derring-do, gaiety, charm and courage, are all the more fantastic because the persons are real, even though they might seem right out of the pages of Hans Christian Andersen.

You will not find dates and statistics here, except where they seem necessary to explain how or why a saint got to his particular spot. And I have used the embroidery of legend because I feel that under its eye-catching trivia, there is the good homespun of fact. Sometimes it has been hard to discover which facts are the real facts. In reading six books about one saint, you may have as many versions of his or her death—he may have died on the battlefield, in the arms of a wife or son, pinned to a tree with seven arrows . . . or a combination of all three.

I have often (but not always!) chosen lesser-known saints because these are the ones to whom I am drawn, coaxing these hideaway saints out of the dusty pages of old reference books for one brief, if fanciful moment in the sun.

—Ethel Pochocki

Francis Xavier

December 3

Once upon a time, a young Spanish nobleman named Francis Xavier dreamed of becoming a famous scholar and philosopher. He would become so well-known that people on the street would whisper and shove and curtsy as he passed by and say to each other, "Look, there goes Francis Xavier, the well-known, handsome, talented, charming scholar whose books are in *all* the libraries of Spain!"

To make this dream come true, he knew he would have to study with all the brains God had given him, and that he did. He went to the University of Paris where he quickly became one of its best students. Here he met a strange man who was very unlike Francis (who *was* handsome, talented, charming, and on his way to becoming well-known). This man, whose name was Ignatius, was a former soldier, older, lame, uncaring as to how he looked (Francis was very fussy about his clothes).

Ignatius would wait in the shadows of the buildings, his stern eyes set in an unsmiling face, and when Francis passed by, he would whisper to him, "Psst! Francis! What does it profit a man if he gains the whole world and loses his soul?"

Not just once, but over and over he did this, until Francis became quite angry. He was upset and did not know why. The words stuck in his mind and would spring out at him when he didn't expect them.

They haunted him, until one day he went to Ignatius and said, "I know you are a holy man and that God is speaking through you to me—but what do you want of me?"

Ignatius told him that he was forming an order of priests called the Society of Jesus and he had chosen Francis to be one of the first seven founders. Francis understood. "Well," he said, "this is one way for you to make sure I don't lose my soul!"

He began to study twice as hard now; and by the time he was 31 years old, he was ordained a priest. He went to Rome to work as Ignatius' letter-writer, so he was the first to open and read an important message from King John of Portugal.

The King asked Ignatius' help in finding priests to go to India to tell the people there everything about Christ, whom they did not know. Ignatius knew he must send Francis, who was his very best worker, and he was sad, knowing that he would probably never see him again in this life. "Go, Francis," he said with tears in his heart, "and set all on fire!"

Francis left for a three-month trip across the Alps and Spain to Portugal, where he would board a boat for the 11,000-mile voyage. He knew it would not be a short trip, but he never dreamed it would be 13 months! Can you imagine not walking on land or even seeing trees or houses for over a year?

The passengers and crew grew very restless. They were frightened, bored, grumpy and, most of all, sick. Most of them had scurvy, which came from eating poor food and not being able to have oranges and tomatoes and grapefruits. Vitamin C pills to take their place hadn't been invented yet. Francis did his best to soothe their fears, referee fights, tell them jokes and, through all of this, let them know that God was watching over them.

They finally arrived on the west coast of India in a town called Goa. Francis worked first among the rough and rude soldiers and colonists who had come from Europe and who no longer followed Christ's teaching. They were giving the native Indians a bad example of how Christians should act.

After convincing most of them to change their lives to let our Lord's light in, Francis went on to the southern coast and spent two years among the native pearl fishermen and their families. He lived as they did: slept on the ground, ate little but rice and water, washed his own clothes and cleaned his own pots. They loved him for this.

He had a funny way of getting people's attention in the villages where he preached. He would go through the streets ringing a little bell and, when the children and mothers came running, he would tell the story of our Lord and his mother in little rhymes, or fit the words to tunes, so they could hum them while they cut hay or mended nets. The little girls would jump rope as they sang:

> Mary had a lit-tle Son,
> > lit-tle Son,
> > lit-tle Son,
> Mary had a lit-tle Son,
> Who came to save us all!

After traveling all over India teaching and baptizing, Francis set sail for the Spice Islands. He loved to offer Mass here, with the heavenly smell of cinnamon and nutmegs and cloves all about him to remind him of the sweetness of Christ's love for all his children. Then he set sail again, this time for Japan.

He found the people and their ways very different from those he had known in India. They did not seem friendly at all. Francis knew he must learn their language and learn it well. It took him a year before he felt sure enough of what he was saying. He certainly didn't want to offend a prospective Christian by calling him a cross-eyed porcupine when what he really wanted to say was, "How do you do, would you like to know how you can live forever?"

Even when he did learn to speak their tongue, the Japanese looked at him with scorn and then turned away so they wouldn't have to look at him at all. Francis sat down one day, scratched and bruised from stones thrown by children, and thought about this situation.

Why, he wondered, didn't he have the love and respect of these people as he did in India? Surely he was the same person. The Holy Spirit gave him a nudge and something clicked in his understanding. The Japanese, being a very proud and respectable people, would not listen to a beggar who wore the same rags day after day, no matter what important message he brought.

He knew what he must do. He dressed in the most handsome robes he could find and, with his fellow priests in attendance like a royal procession, he presented himself to the ruler as a prince from Portugal. He gave the monarch an armful of gifts—a music box, a pair of velvet slippers, a cuckoo clock and a letter from King John, explaining who he was and why he was here.

The ruler was so pleased with this royal treatment he immediately gave the visitor permission to teach anywhere in his country and an old temple to live in. Once he had been accepted by them, Francis found the Japanese people to be gentle, gracious and nature-loving. They became Christians and friends. Often they asked him why he had come to Japan instead of China, since China was the most important "Forbidden Empire."

Francis felt it was time for him to go to China. But everything seemed to stand in his way. "You may be sure of one thing," he wrote to a friend, "the devil will be very sorry to see the Society of Jesus enter China, judging by the obstacles he puts in my way every day."

He persisted. Finally a friend told him of a Chinese pirate who would smuggle him into Canton. Francis waited for him on the hot, desolate, windswept island of Sanchian, off the China coast, for three months. But the pirate never came. Francis caught a fever and then a chill. He had wanted to get to China so badly, but our Lord must have felt that Francis had already done more than one saint should do. China must be left for the missionaries to come.

As he lay on the island shore in sand that burned his skin, he felt a touch cool as rainwater on his eyes. "Never mind, Francis," said a pleasant, pleased voice. "Think of all those happy people who know my Son because of you. Now don't fret over China. Just close your eyes, it's time to come home."

And he did.

Prayer of a Would-be Saint

with heart serene
and cheerful face
with will and wit
and God's good grace

let me
do what I can
where I am
with what I have

Nicholas

December 6

Once upon a time in the country of Lycia, there lived a saint called Nicholas who is said to have worked a miracle the day he was born. As his nurse was giving him his first bath, he stood up straight, clasped his hands and looked up to heaven. Now, it takes some months before a baby can crawl or hold onto something, much less stand right up. So when Nicholas did this, everyone there knew that this was a very special baby.

He grew up as a happy child in a loving and comfortable family. They had more than enough of everything; perhaps that is why Nicholas never thought about money, or about holding on to it. He shared his marbles and graham crackers as easily as breathing, and if a friend said, "My, that's a good-looking shirt," he would take it right off and give it to him.

And once he gave something, he never stood around watching to make sure the person used it wisely. "Once you give a gift, let it go," he would say. "It is no longer yours, so go and tend to your own business."

When Nicholas was a young man, his parents died and left him a large fortune, and he made it his business to give it away. Not all at once in one big lump, but in his own way. Besides giving presents, Nicholas loved planning secret surprises. If he had been born at another time to other parents, he might have become an actor.

Instead, he used all his talents along with his wealth to live as a mysterious gift-giver. He would ride through town in the night, his cloak flying in the wind, a silk mask over his eyes, throwing a little bag of gold pieces through a window or doorway, or leaving it in the milk bottle on the porch, and then ride back off into the dark.

For years he did this, seeking out those who had the most need—a father who needed money to marry off his daughters, a farmer who needed a new ox, a widow who needed oatmeal and raisins for her children. He would see to it that they got the gold to take care of their needs. And he gave presents to children that weren't really needed but which made their eyes crinkle with joy and their feet jump up and down—almonds and oranges and silk scarves and calico kittens with blue eyes and Tootsie Rolls. Wouldn't he have made the nicest uncle who would come visiting with pockets crammed with such things?

We know that Nicholas must have been found out, for on his feast day, it is the custom in many countries to put your shoes outside your door the night before, and by morning St. Nicholas will have filled them with goodies. We carry on the custom by hanging up our Christmas stockings the night before our Lord is born, "in the hopes that St. Nicholas soon will be there." And he is bound to be there, for anyone who loves children and gifts and surprises as much as Nicholas would never miss *this* birthday!

When all Nicholas' money had been given away, Nicholas said, "Now I can become a priest and give away *more* than money." The first thing he did once he was a priest was to make a pilgrimage to the Holy Land, and he had to do this by boat. On the second day

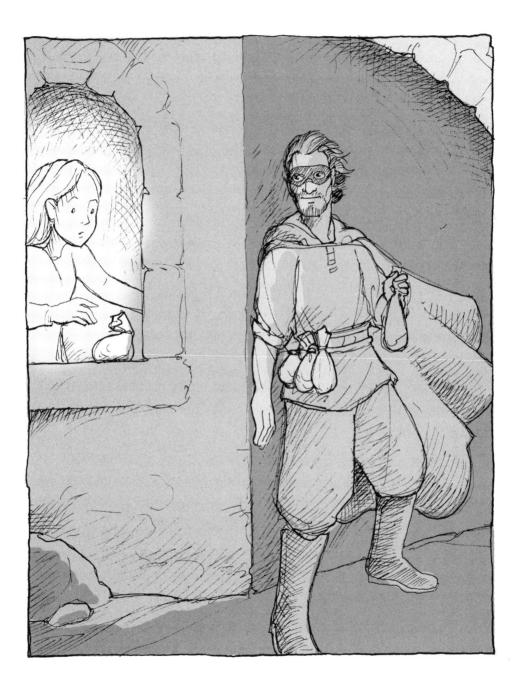

out, when Nicholas was still trying not to be seasick, a ferocious storm grabbed the boat and tossed it about the waves like an empty cracker box.

The old captain, who had weathered many storms, had never seen such a tempest as this. He and the crew grabbed onto anything fastened down and held on for dear life. Nicholas knelt down on the tilting deck, raised his eyes to heaven and prayed that they be saved. "I've only just begun, Lord, I have so much more to do!"

The captain yelled above the roar of the wind, "What good are prayers now? Don't waste your breath! I'm going to tie you to the mast before you're swept over—"

Just then, the waves stopped churning, the black sky lightened and the sun began to shine so brightly it made rainbows in drops of water everywhere. Nicholas said, "You see, nothing is ever past praying for!"

And from that time, Nicholas has been the friend of sailors. Sometimes in the wildest of storms, sailors swear that they have seen him kneeling on the deck, with his arms outstretched as if to protect them.

Nicholas was such a good priest he soon became a bishop. His first love, after God, was for children. He would seek them out as he traveled the land to help them, protect them and sometimes even rescue them. Once in a town near his home, three little boys wandered off and got lost. They kept walking and soon came to a neat pleasant-looking inn. It was painted gray and had red shutters and a sign over the gate that read: Dew Drop Inn. So they said, "Let's!" And they did.

The innkeeper listened to their story of being lost and said of course he would be *glad* to put them up for the night. He rubbed his hands together and smiled so hard you couldn't see his eyes. The boys were happy that they had found such a nice, understanding person but, as you will see, he was not really nice.

He was the kind of person who could look at three little boys and think how good they would be served up roasted, on a platter with three bright red apples in their mouths. Or better yet, chopped up, put into a salty brine and pickled like pigs' feet.

Would you believe that this wicked man put his thoughts into action? By the next morning, the little boys were on their way to becoming pickles.

That very night, Nicholas had a nightmare which made him sit up in bed and count the thumpbeats of his heart. He had dreamed that three little boys had been chopped up and put into a tub of salty brine at the very inn he passed on his way to church.

In the morning, he dressed quickly and went straight to the inn. The innkeeper was taken by surprise for it wasn't even seven o'clock yet. But he smiled and rubbed his hands greedily. Bishops were rich, he had heard, and people said this one was always giving away money, so he'd better be extra nice.

"Ah, Your Eminence," he bowed low, "Your Royal Churchly Excellency, what can this humble inn possibly offer you in keeping with your absolutely, perfectly presumptuous holy person? Ham and eggs? Sausage and pancakes? Cream of wheat?"

"How about," said Nicholas slowly, "some pickled pigs' feet? I woke this morning with an overwhelming craving you wouldn't believe. Isn't that some over there?" And he pointed to the old wooden tub with the boys in the brine.

The innkeeper grew very pale. "Oh no, Sir, Your Most Admirable Royalness, that's not ready yet."

"Why not?" asked Nicholas, rising slowly and towering over the quaking man. "Is it because it is too fresh? Is it because there are no pigs' feet in there, only three little boys chopped up?"

The innkeeper fell to his knees, shaking and wailing. He had been found out. What would happen to him? Nicholas went to the tub, raised his eyes to heaven and made the Sign of the Cross over the bits and pieces buried under the brine.

The water bubbled a little, as if something were stirring around at the bottom, and then up popped three very wet little heads. They smiled at the bishop and all three said in one voice: "What a marvelous sleep I've had!"

The innkeeper fainted from the shock. When he came to, he knelt down with Nicholas and the boys and prayed for forgiveness. From that day on, the innkeeper never again gave customers the wrong change, or stole money from the pockets of sleeping guests, or served pickled pigs' feet unless they were just that.

Our Lady of Guadalupe

December 12

When Mary decides now and then to visit us on earth, the stories of these appearances delight every part of us that loves fantasy. They are the loveliest of fairy tales—except that they aren't fairy tales, they are *real*. This is the story of one of those visits, in which Mary came as Our Lady of Guadalupe and gave us "the miracle of the roses."

She came for a few days in December 1531 to a hill a few miles outside of Mexico City. Ten years earlier, the Spaniards had conquered Mexico and were trying to convert the native Aztec Indians to Christianity, sometimes by force. The Franciscan priests who had come with the armies told them it was cruel to punish and harm the Indians because they worshipped God differently. But the Spaniards did not want to hear this.

So it was not a good time for the Indians. Even those who converted were often treated no better than servants. Among these was Juan Diego, a fifty-seven-year-old widower, who lived with his elderly uncle, also named Juan. They lived a life of meager comforts in a hut with a thatched roof; yet gentle Juan Diego did not complain. He loved the simple joys which this new Christian God had given him—sun and wind and birdsong and the day's needs. He had no great aspirations, no secret sorrows or great anger. He considered himself quite small in the scheme of things, and he didn't mind that at all.

On a cold December morning, he set off at daybreak for Mass, going his usual route past a small hill called Tepeyac, which had once been a shrine to the Aztec Mother Goddess. He wrapped his cloak tightly about him and walked with his head bent into the stinging cold wind. Suddenly he stopped. He thought he heard birds singing, so sweetly that he thought his heart would melt.

But this was not possible. Birdsong in bleak December? But it continued, now a full chorus of different voices. It was coming from the top of Tepeyac, where the sky was lit with a strange glow. Being ever curious, he climbed toward it. He stopped when he reached the top, frozen at the sight before him.

A beautiful young Indian woman stood in the center of a globe of golden light, from which fingers of rainbows spread out in rays. Her dark hair hung softly around her round face with olive skin and green eyes that looked compassionately at him. Her head was tilted slightly to the right. Juan thought she must be a queen, with her long rose-colored robe and turquoise mantle bordered in gold and scattered with golden stars.

Not only the Lady, but also everything around her glittered— the ground on which she stood seemed dusted with diamonds, and all the cactus and thistle and weed plants sparkled like emeralds. Everything seemed enchanted. Juan wondered if he was in heaven, but he didn't remember dying, so he didn't think so.

The songs of the birds ceased, and the woman spoke. "Juan? Juanito, my little one, come closer so you may hear me."

Juan Diego did as she asked. Even though he was speechless, he was not frightened. "Juan," the Lady said, "I am the ever-Virgin,

Holy Mary, Mother of the true God, the Lord of heaven and earth. I have come to ask a favor of you. I want you to be my ambassador. Will you go to the bishop and tell him I wish him to build a church here, so I may give all my love and help to you and your people? My people. I am your mother and the mother of all who cry to and need me. Listen, my son, go now to the bishop and tell him what I desire. Tell him what you have seen. Go quickly, and do not tarry!"

Juan Diego, his heart pounding, said yes, he would go, and left immediately. *Now* he was frightened. He knew how foolish he, a timid peasant, would look and sound to the bishop, but he would not, could not, refuse this Lady anything, for the Holy Mother of heaven had come down and spoken to him in his native Aztec tongue. She must truly love him.

When Juan arrived at the bishop's palace, he had to wait for hours to see him for, as he expected, no one thought a peasant had anything of importance to tell His Eminence. Finally he was shown into the presence of Bishop Juan de Zumarraga, a Franciscan priest who had come to Mexico three years before. Like the Spanish soldiers, he was a firm, no-nonsense, powerful man, but unlike them, he was merciful and tried to lessen their cruel treatment of the Indians.

He listened politely to Diego, who went on and on telling some strange story in his native Aztec. The bishop thought the poor old fellow was probably off his rocker, talking about seeing the Queen of Heaven on Tepeyac Hill. He thanked Juan for sharing this news with him, asked him to visit him again sometime and dismissed him.

Juan was disappointed but not surprised. Why should the bishop believe him? He arrived back at Tepeyac just as the sun was setting and found the Lady awaiting him. He told her what had happened with the bishop—nothing. "Why don't you choose someone else," he asked her, "someone the bishop respects? He thinks I am just a crazy Indian. I am a nobody, a small rope, a tiny ladder, a leaf. . . ."

The Lady interrupted him. "My son, I have chosen you to carry my wishes to the bishop. You are *not* a nobody. You must try again. Tell the bishop that you come in my name, that the Mother of God has sent you, and he is to build a church for my people."

The next morning, Juan Diego went once again to Mexico City, and waited to see the bishop. This time the bishop listened, cautiously. There was something about this Indian, his innocence, his intense sincerity, the joy with which he described the Lady, that made him wonder if there could be truth in all this.

He questioned Juan in more detail: How many stars were on her robe? Did she stand on the ground or float above it? Did she hold her hands out? Were there any angels? Juan repeated his story and left nothing out. Finally the bishop said that Juan should ask for a sign from the Lady as proof she was truly the Mother of God, and then he would build the church.

As soon as Juan left, the bishop ordered two of his servants to follow him and report back on what he did and where he went. But as they approached Tepeyac, they lost sight of him as if he had disappeared into the air, and they had to return with nothing to tell the bishop.

Meanwhile, Juan had already given the Lady the bishop's request for a sign. She nodded and smiled and said, "Come back tomorrow, my son, and you shall have it. Go, and rest now."

Juan Diego hoped the bishop would come to his senses soon, because he was getting tired of walking ten miles each day in this bitter cold.

But he did not come the next morning because his uncle was very ill, near death he feared, and he spent the day staying home and taking care of him. At daybreak the next day, his uncle seemed worse and begged him to get the priest to hear his confession. Juan started off immediately, but in a different direction, away from Tepeyac Hill. He did not want to meet the Lady now, for she would detain him. He would explain to her later, he told himself.

But suddenly, there she was, right in the middle of the path waiting for him! (This just shows, in case you didn't already know, that mothers can never be outwitted.) "Juanito, little one, what's wrong?" she asked gently, as he stood in awkward silence. Now he was worried about his uncle dying without the sacrament *and* ashamed of trying to avoid her, but she smiled and reassured him she understood.

"Don't worry about your uncle. He will recover and be better than ever. Now, if you will please go back to Tepeyac, you will find all the proof you need for the bishop. There will be roses at the top of the hill, many kinds. Pick all you can carry."

Juan obeyed but found this almost too much to believe. Roses in December? Growing out of this frozen solid, snow-covered ground? But he climbed the hill and found exactly that. More roses than he could possibly pick, not just *ordinary* lovely roses but a rare and

gorgeous variety found in the gardens of Castile, Spain, a kind the bishop would surely know. The petals were covered with a morning dew that did not freeze.

He gathered as many as his cloak would hold and brought them to the Lady, who arranged them in a manner which suited her and wrapped them in a fold of the cloak so they could not be seen. (This cloak is called a *tilma* in Mexico, and every native wore one. Besides keeping warm in them, men used them as sacks to carry food from the market, and women wrapped their babies in them so they would be safe and warm.)

"There, now," said the Lady, satisfied. "Here is the bishop's proof. Tell him how you came by them, at my order, and he will see in them my wish and he will comply with it."

When Juan reached the palace, his precious, fragrant bounty covered tightly in his *tilma*, he was not kept waiting. The perfume of the roses followed him into the bishop's presence. Juan knelt before him, opened his *tilma* and let the roses fall to the floor. The bishop gasped, not only at the sight of the roses but also at another miracle Juan didn't know about.

On Juan Diego's *tilma* was a life-sized, brilliantly colored painting of the Lady, just as he had seen her, right down to the slight tilt of her head. The gentle green eyes gave the same reassurance that all would be well.

The bishop fell to his knees beside Juan Diego, who was quite surprised that he had been wearing such a thing of beauty. He knew no one could have painted it because he had been wearing it. He hoped the bishop wouldn't want proof about this too!

Fortunately, the bishop now knew that Mary had truly sent this humble man as her special messenger and he treated Juan as such. Juan was given another cloak, one of real warmth, and spent the day at the palace. The next day he and the bishop went to Tepeyac Hill to the spot where the Lady had asked a church be built. The bishop ordered a chapel built, beginning that very day, which would be dedicated to Our Lady of Guadalupe, which was a village in Spain. Juan Diego's *tilma* was hung over the altar, and hundreds, then thousands, of people came to see the miraculous image of the Lady, the mother of the Christian God, who had come down to speak to one of their own in their native tongue.

But that's not the end of the miracle. It continues today. The painting of Our Lady of Guadalupe still hangs above the altar of the church dedicated to her, which is no longer a chapel but a grand basilica. People make pilgrimages there by the millions to ask her help or thank her for their own personal miracles.

The painting has not faded, cracked or peeled in the 463 years since Juan Diego dropped it at the bishop's feet, nor has the material of the *tilma*, made from fibers of the cactus plant, fallen apart. Scientists and chemists cannot identify the paint used. Art experts say there is no evidence of a human hand in the painting, no brushstrokes, no sketches underneath. After years and years of research, the only answer is that it is a mystery, an unexplainable miracle.

Perhaps the simplest miracle, that which impressed the native Indians and converted them wholeheartedly to Christianity, was the idea of a God whose mother showed such gracious courtesy in coming to them and speaking to them as one of their own. How could they not believe in a God with such a caring mother?

Our Lady of Guadalupe,
who gives believers
in fairy tales and miracles
reason to rejoice,
wrap us royally
in stars and moon
and mothercare strong
as spider silk,
as we plod numbly
through the snow
in shivering quest.
Warm our hearts
with certainty
that you will bring
roses to our winter,
that even as we ask,
we smell their fragrance!

Lucy

December 13

Not too long after Jesus' time, in the country of Sicily there lived a bright little girl named Lucy. Her name comes from the Latin word *lux*, which means light, and she was indeed one of the brightest lights of the early Church.

She spent a happy childhood as the apple of everyone's eye, especially her parents'. When her father died, her life changed, but her sunny manner did not. True to her name, she tried to look on the bright side of things. She helped cheer her mother who had become sad and sickly now that her husband was gone.

She would fluff her mother's pillows and brush her hair as she talked. "Mother, you know Daddy is in heaven, so why do you cry? We'll be there with him someday. We just have to be patient." They knew death was not the end of everything because they were Christians, and Christians were often close to death, for it was a crime in those days to follow Christ.

Her mother agreed and tried to think happy thoughts, but she seemed to grow worse. Soon she could not even walk. She had to be carried about or pushed around in a wheelchair. Lucy had a dream in which St. Agatha told her to go to her tomb 50 miles away to pray for a cure for her mother. Lucy told her mother, and they both felt it would be good for them to get out of the house and make the trip. Maybe, just maybe, if it were God's will, her mother would soon be well.

After three days of walking and pushing the wheelchair up and down hills, they reached St. Agatha's tomb. It was quite late and they quickly fell asleep. Again, the saint appeared to Lucy in a dream and this time told her that her mother would be healed.

When Lucy woke the next day, sure enough it had happened! Her mother was already up. She stretched, braided her own hair, and declared she hadn't felt better in years. She left the wheelchair for someone who might need it and walked home so briskly Lucy had a hard time keeping up with her.

Lucy had been thinking about something very important since her father died and decided to tell her mother about it now. "I want to give the money Father gave me to all the people who have less than we do, Mother. I want to be poor as Jesus was. And another thing. I really don't want to marry the nice young man you chose for me. He is well-off, I know, but he will never believe as we do. Besides, I want to follow Jesus and no other man."

Her mother was so happy and grateful to Lucy for taking her to be cured that she would grant her anything. "You may do as you wish, Lucy dear, but I do hope your fiancé won't be too upset."

But he *was* very upset, and not at all as nice as Lucy had thought. "If I can't have Lucy, then no one shall," he snarled spitefully, and he went to the Governor to turn her in.

"Lucy is a Christian and worships a strange God instead of our Roman ones," he told him. The Governor ordered that Lucy must be killed in the manner of the day. That meant she would be tied

to the horns of two mean-tempered bulls and dragged through the streets as a warning to other Christians.

So they bound Lucy's hands and ankles tight and tied two leather ropes around her waist. The other ends of the ropes were tied to the bulls' horns. The soldiers cracked their whips across the bulls' backs and the angry beasts charged down the street, snorting and tossing their heads. But Lucy remained on her spot as if rooted in cement. The leather ropes snapped and the bulls raced off to nowhere in clouds of dust.

The soldiers tried again, this time with two wild-eyed stallions, and the same thing happened. The crowd was muttering. They had come to see a young Christian put to death, and here she stood, hands and feet bound, gazing off into the sky and humming to herself. They pushed her and tore at her robe and stepped on her toes, but still they could not budge her from the spot.

"Enough of this," growled the Governor, who was greatly irritated by this stubborn girl. He ran into the street, drew out his sword, and plunged it into Lucy's throat. She went to heaven immediately, where Jesus was waiting to welcome her and show her about her new home.

To this day, Lucy doesn't forget those who need her on earth. All over the world people with sore eyes pray for her to send down her "lucy-light" to help them see better, and anyone with a sore throat would, as you can imagine, find her very sympathetic.

In Sweden she is the patron of schoolgirls. On her feast day, little girls in Sweden and Norway wear a crown of candles and flowers in their hair and, as a special treat, bring their mothers breakfast in bed.

If you lived in Hungary, you would plant a few grains of wheat on Lucy's feast day so that you would have a pot of new green sprouts by Christmas. This is to remind us that we never ever die. Like the winter wheat and Lucy, when we seem to "die," we are really reborn into another life, as full of untold delight as God has promised.

The Holy Innocents

December 28

Once upon a time on a December day in Bethlehem, something very sad happened because someone very wonderful had been born on Christmas Day. Many children, little boys two years old and younger, were killed by an incredibly evil king named Herod.

When someone is incredibly evil, we try to understand how he became that way. But Herod was so bad (he even killed four of his own sons), perhaps we had best leave him to God to figure out. I certainly would not like to be in *his* sandals on Judgment Day.

But we do wonder what kind of person could take the lives of these Holy Innocents, as they are called, who hadn't even had time to learn to be bad. *Innocents* are those who can do no wrong or harm because they don't know what they are doing.

Yet Herod was afraid of one such child who would take his throne and then Herod would no longer be King. Already three kings had arrived at his palace, traveling from a country in the East, asking, "Where is he who has been born King of the Jews? For we have seen his star in the East and have come to worship him."

This made the King terribly nervous. He was impressed with their kingly robes and servants and mysterious jeweled boxes which he suspected held presents for someone royal.

Herod called together his wise men and fortune-tellers and asked

them where this baby, this new King, had been born. And they told him, "In Bethlehem." So Herod thought up a clever plan.

He called the Magi into his living room and offered them cigars and chocolate-covered mints and said he hoped they would have a pleasant journey to Bethlehem.

"Oh, and by the way," he added quickly, "When you find this young child, please come back and bring me news of him, so I may go and worship him also."

The three kings followed their star to the stable and gave their gifts to Jesus and Mary. They spent the night in a cave nearby since the stable was already so crowded. In their dreams that night, an angel warned each of them that Herod was not to be trusted and wanted to kill the Infant King. So they took a different road home the next morning and never returned to Herod's palace.

That same night, an angel warned Joseph about Herod and told him to get up quickly, to take Mary and Jesus and to leave for Egypt immediately. This they did.

Herod waited and waited for the three kings to return. Finally his fortune-tellers told him that he had been tricked. The Magi were already on their way back home. Herod became so angry he turned red and then purple. His eyes bulged with hate.

"I will not be mocked by a mere baby. If I don't know which one to kill, I will kill them *all*. I will be free of this bothersome worry and be King forever!" He clenched his fists and screamed for his soldiers.

He ordered them to kill every boy two years old and younger in Bethlehem and the surrounding village. Again, he thought up a clever trick and a cruel one. He knew if the mothers knew what he was up to, they would run in all directions trying to hide their children, and the soldiers couldn't go every which way at once. One would be bound to escape and it could be the Infant King.

So Herod invited the mothers to gather in the public square for a party to celebrate the birth of his own new son. Everyone was excited, for a party meant a chance to exchange stories of their children and wear their best clothes and eat a cake baked by someone else. So they bathed their sons and brushed their hair and told them to mind their manners.

It was a terrible moment when Herod's soldiers came and took their children from them and carried out the King's orders. If you, right now, can feel sadness in reading this, can you imagine how much more sorrow filled the hearts of those mothers?

Bethlehem was now a town with only little girls. There were no sounds of little boys chasing each other in and out of each other's houses, or making roads with their toy trucks, or playing ball with their fathers after supper.

The only thought that gave comfort to the young mothers was that one child did escape the one whom Herod feared. For all his wise men and fortune-tellers and soldiers, Herod had no power to compare with that of angels' warnings and God's will.

The Holy Innocents were the first martyrs, the "flower buds nipped by frost" for Christ's sake. These little ones did not die for Christ because they knew what they were doing. They died because they were there and *could* have been Christ. They died, but our Lord lived, and because he lived, none of us shall ever die.

The next time your two-year-old brother scribbles with red crayon on your homework, or dumps his orange juice *again*, don't swat him or yell for your mother to *do* something with him. Just remember that he is an *Innocent* whom God gave to your family as a special gift. And put away your crayons.

Elizabeth Seton

January 4

There was once a little girl who became a saint by *looking up*. She didn't spend her life flying kites, or plastering ceilings, or searching the sky for geese in spring. Her *looking-up* was a bigger, grander thing. It was a great umbrella which covered every happening of her life.

Her name was Elizabeth Ann Bayley, and she was born into a wealthy Episcopalian family in New York City in 1774. It was an exciting time to come into the world, for our country itself would be born in two years and New York City would be its first capital. Hearts were filled with hope and quick to promise the hard work needed for true independence.

Elizabeth's story, as the years went by, was like that of the American pioneers who were stalwart in hardship, ever pressing on to their goal. But her goal was not to reach an outpost in the northern wilds or a settlement in the desert. It was to do God's will wherever he put her.

She didn't think of such things as she grew up amid the comforts and pleasures enjoyed by well-to-do young ladies in New York society. Elizabeth was properly proficient in French and music and good manners. She went to the theater and read the latest novels and went shopping for ball gowns and Swiss chocolates. She dutifully read her daily Scripture and went to Trinity Episcopal Church on

Sunday, but she wasn't extraordinarily pious. Every now and then she would dramatically announce that she wanted to join the Quakers. And when shocked friends would ask why on earth *why*, she would laugh, "Because they have such pretty little bonnets!"

When she went to parties, all the young men had their eyes on the charming Miss Bayley with the merry brown eyes. But these brown eyes could see only one man. His name was William Magee Seton. His family owned a shipping firm and was also wealthy. Both families were delighted at the thought of such a match. Such a handsome pair—they were made for each other!

Elizabeth and William felt they were too, so at the age of 19 she became Mrs. William Seton. They began their life together in a mansion, one of the many which lined Wall Street in New York City, and William joined his father in the business. Life was heavenly and Elizabeth dreamed that all their life would be sweet. They would raise a family, she and Will, and go to church on Sunday. And she would do charity work on Thursday and have a Literary Tea on Monday. And in the evening, when the children were in bed, she would sew or read while Will played his Stradivarius violin, which he would make sing with his touch. Her world was perfect, and she had no wish to change it. But God did.

It began when her father-in-law died and Will had to take over the business. It did not go well. Ships were lost to storms at sea or were taken by pirates. Will would fret and worry as the fortune slipped away. Elizabeth took care of the books and tried to pay the bills, but try as they might to keep it going, the business failed.

The young couple felt the first pinch of hardship. They moved to a smaller house and began selling furniture to buy food for the family. Creditors banged on the door, demanding their payment. Will was depressed and could not find work. Elizabeth would try to cheer him and he would hug her tightly, calling her his "old knot of oak."

He began to cough and grow thinner and weaker each day. What Elizabeth feared was true: He had tuberculosis and needed much rest. Her father, who was a doctor, worried that she and the children (by now there were five) would also catch some disease in the crowded city, so the family spent the summer with Dr. Bayley on Long Island.

At that time, Dr. Bayley was the health officer for the city of New York. His work was to examine the newly-arrived immigrants from Ireland. Elizabeth went with him to help, and her heart was saddened by the condition of the newcomers. She had never seen such sickness and hunger and pinched, gaunt cheeks. But she saw no despair. The name of God was on the immigrants' tongues and rosaries rubbed to a shine were wound around the hands of young and old. How strong was the faith of these immigrants!

They were coming into a land of opportunity—and disease. The dreaded yellow fever was an epidemic in New York. Dr. Bayley had tried in vain to clean up the stagnant swamps around the city and the mounds of garbage where the germs bred. But by the end of that summer, he too caught the fever and died.

Elizabeth was numb with grief. Then her husband took a turn for the worse. The young wife remembered the Psalms she had read in her childhood. Bit by bit they came back to her and put her heart at peace. "I have become a *looker-up*," she told her children "We shall not worry. God will get us through and Daddy will get better and we shall be a family as we used to be once again."

A sea journey was what Will needed, she decided. The fresh salty air, the clear sky, rest—that would do it. So she sold the house and her family possessions—the silver, the crystal, even the gold locket with her mother's picture. The one thing she could not bear to sell was Will's violin, which she gave to a friend for safekeeping. Anna, the oldest, went with them, but William, Richard, Catherine and Rebecca, who were too young, stayed at home.

Will coughed less and seemed stronger during the voyage. When they saw the green hills of Italy coming into view, their spirits were high. Will was getting better and they would be staying with the Setons' good friends, the Filicchi family. Antonio Filicchi was waiting at the dock, waving, and they hurried to leave the ship and join him. Suddenly a sailor blocked their way and refused to let them off. They were to be kept in quarantine until it was certain they had not brought in any yellow fever germs from New York.

For 40 days they were kept on an island in a stone, prison-like building called the Lazaretto. Elizabeth remembered the immigrants from Ireland for whom she had felt such pity. Now she knew how they had felt. The Setons' room had nothing: no heat, bed, chairs, food—nothing. A mattress was brought in for Will. The wind from the sea whistled and whined through a crack in the wall. Elizabeth looked up and asked, "Lord, please do something!"

Antonio showed up the next day, as welcome as a guardian angel. He brought blankets, food, wood, some wine—even curtains and some toys for Anna and a servant, Luigi. Luigi ran errands, brought medicine, tended the fire. Will no longer seemed to be improving, but Elizabeth hid her fears from Anna. Together they played games and jumped rope to keep warm.

When they were finally allowed to leave two weeks before Christmas, Will was a shivering bag of bones, sicker than ever. The Filicchis took the tenderest care of their friend, but it was too late. Two days after Christmas, Will's tired heart stopped beating and he died. Elizabeth was now a widow.

The Filicchis tried to cheer her with trips to the city to visit art museums and churches. When they invited her to go to Mass with them she accepted, curious about this religion that seemed as important to her wealthy Italian friends as it was to the poor Irish immigrants. When she knelt before the Blessed Sacrament, she was filled with a peace she had not known before. She felt a turning inside her, a giving over of her soul which she called "an entire surrender of itself and all its faculties to God."

Despite the kindness of the Filicchi family and the new spiritual questioning within her heart, Elizabeth was at a crossroads and knew that she must return home to find her way. Here she sat, a young widow, penniless in a foreign country. What would she do? Where would she go? Why had God allowed this to happen?

Deep in her soul, she knew there was a reason. She had enough faith, even then, to look up and to trust that out of the worst comes the best. "Afflictions," she later wrote, "are the steps to heaven. Have confidence! Never let the comparison of time and eternity slip an instant from your mind. I find this cures all sorrow."

Elizabeth decided to leave Italy and get on with a life for herself and her children. How she missed them! As she and Anna boarded the ship to America, Antonio hugged her and said, "Never fear, my child. God, who takes care of the birds and lilies, will take care of you, too!"

Four healthy and happy children awaited them in New York. The first thing Elizabeth did was find a small apartment in the house of a friend. Then she decided to open a school for girls in her home. Parents were only too happy to send students to lovely Mrs. Seton who had known such tragedy. She was soon making a fair living and was even able to buy some treats for the children and books for herself.

Elizabeth began to think more and more about the Catholic faith. She went to her minister at Trinity Church for advice. He was very shocked and not at all sympathetic. In fact, he was quite angry.

"I told you those Catholics in Italy would poison your mind! You must stay away from them and their religion. I tell you, if you become a Catholic I will have nothing more to do with you!"

So Elizabeth did nothing for a year but pray and wonder and worry. A letter from Antonio urged her to study both religions to find the truth for herself. "Whatever you do," he wrote, "I am your friend forever." So she studied and, finally, one day in March, 1804, she walked into St. Peter's church on Barclay Street and told the priest, "I want to become a Catholic."

These words changed Elizabeth's life. Her relatives, except for her sisters-in-law Cecilia and Harriet (who would one day follow her into the Church), would have nothing more to do with her or her children. "How could any intelligent, well-bred woman make such a mistake? And those poor little children, she'll probably make Catholics out of them, too!" Elizabeth Seton was a good topic of gossip at many afternoon teas.

Parents immediately took their children out of her school and she soon was running out of money. She gathered her children around her and hugged them. "Well, my loves, it seems we are off on another adventure. Never mind. Don't sniffle, Rebecca. God is with us, so what shall we fear? We won't look behind or before, only *up*."

Where would they go? The Filicchis had invited them to come to Italy, but Elizabeth felt she should stay in America since it was her home. Then she received a letter from a priest in Baltimore, Maryland, asking if she would come there since they were very much in need of Catholic teachers. He would also provide a home for her at the school.

Baltimore! It was so far from New York, from all she knew. But Elizabeth trusted in God's direction. She would go with complete, accepting enthusiasm. She wrote, "I am gently, quietly, silently a Catholic; the difficulties are all past; only a few knotty ones there are who must talk of something, and the worst they say is: 'So much trouble has turned her brain.' . . . At all events, happen now what will, I rest in God."

On a sunny June morning Elizabeth set sail down the coast to Baltimore with her three daughters (the boys were away at boarding school) and Harriet and Cecilia. They were welcomed by the priest on their arrival and given a red brick house—"a neat, delightful mansion with folding windows"—where they would live and teach

school. Here they lived for a year while Elizabeth wrestled with another question. She wanted to become a nun. But how could she, with three young daughters still living with her?

Bishop John Carroll, who had confirmed her in New York, gave her permission not only to become a nun, but also to start a new community similar to the one founded by St. Vincent de Paul in France. It would be called the Sisters of Charity.

And so Elizabeth (now called Mother Seton), her new community of seven sisters plus her three daughters left Baltimore for their new home 50 miles away in Emmitsburg. They set off in a covered wagon piled high with mattresses, chairs, pots and pans, lanterns, candles, soaps, linens and, packed very carefully on top, Will's violin, with which Elizabeth would never part.

The wagon bumped and jogged along for three days until they reached their log-cabin home on the side of the mountain. Here they lived until their new home was built. The sisters met the adventure with high spirits. Elizabeth writes of walking to the mountain church: "There was no bridge over the creek . . . and when the water was high, we had to cross one by one on horseback; when it was low, we passed over the stones . . . ." Sometimes Elizabeth would sit on "her" rock and teach catechism to the children of the parish.

The first winter in their new home, which they called the Stone House, was a hard one. The snow often sifted down on the sisters through the roof as they slept. Food was in short supply and they survived on what Providence sent. Sometimes it wasn't what they felt like eating, but Elizabeth, with her way of stirring up fun, made light of the scanty cupboards. If someone gave them a bushel of turnips, she would pretend she had to make a serious decision.

"Now what shall we have for supper tonight? Cream of turnip soup with a dash of nutmeg? Followed by mashed turnip cakes with caraway seed? Followed by a dessert of turnip and dried apple pudding and carrot-top coffee?"

The sisters would groan and Elizabeth would laugh. "Cheer up, it could be a bushel of horseradish. Or sauerkraut!"

Spring came, and the sisters planted a garden and bought chickens and pigs and a cow. Their spirits thrived and so did their school, which Elizabeth called St. Joseph's Free School. Both black and white children attended and, since most were poor, Elizabeth made sure they had snacks of apples and cookies and milk each day.

That stone house was the first Catholic parochial school in the United States. Soon so many pupils came that the sisters had to build a larger school and then a convent to train novices so they might go out to other cities and teach. The Bishop of Philadelphia asked her to send nuns to open the first Catholic orphanage there, and three nuns were requested for the same purpose in New York City. All this happened within two years after Elizabeth sailed out of New York City.

Her personal life was filled with comings and goings of a sadder sort. Her son Richard was lost at sea. Her devoted sisters-in-law, Harriet and Cecilia, died within a few months of each other. They were followed a few years later in death by her daughters Anna and Rebecca. All were buried by a large oak in the cemetery at St.

Joseph's School. Elizabeth, who died at the age of 46, lies near them, buried within the chapel close by.

In her short life Elizabeth Seton was Episcopalian society belle, wife, mother, teacher and Catholic nun. She never lost sight of her goal: to do God's will. And she never tired of *looking up*.

John Neumann

January 5

This is the story of a little man who had a gigantic dream. He was not especially handsome or charming; he had no important friends or family, little money or encouragement. Everything about him was ordinary. He looked like the man who sells mousetraps in the back of the hardware store or who mops the floor of the market at closing time—the kind of man you look at but don't see. Yet, by God's grace, he became the bishop of the city of Philadelphia.

This good, plain man, God's little acorn, was John Neumann. He was born in Bohemia (now part of Czechoslovakia) in 1811. He was a good child who neither caused trouble nor raised high expectations. No one was surprised when he entered the seminary to become a good, plain priest. He studied and studied and found he had a way with words and languages. By the time he was ready to become a priest, he could speak French, German, English and Italian, as well as Latin and Greek. In later years, when he was in America, he would add Gaelic to the list.

John was very short. Even when he was full-grown, he barely reached five feet, two inches. As for the rest of him, he had a broad face and the large, work-worn hands of a farmer. His manner was pleasant and quiet, but underneath this surface was the determination to make real the dream God had given him: to travel to America and minister to the German immigrants. Many people were leaving

43

Germany for America, and John sympathized with these uprooted plants trying to put down new roots in a strange land. They needed the comfort and caring of a spiritual advisor with whom they could talk in their mother tongue, he felt, someone with whom to share old memories and new problems.

He waited eagerly for his ordination day. To his disappointment it had to be delayed because the bishop was ill. So he decided he would go to America and be ordained there. Why waste time?

Thus on a winter's day, he said good-bye to his family, trying not to think that he probably would not see them again. He hugged his mother one more time, wiped away his tears and climbed aboard the stagecoach.

After a rough, joggling trip of 50 days, he arrived in Paris with $40 in his pocket. Here he lived as his money slowly melted away, waiting for answers to his applications to serve in the United States. For months he waited with no response. Finally one day in 1835, an envelope stamped *New York* arrived and John was overjoyed. He had been accepted as an assistant in a parish in Buffalo!

Within the week he set sail on a three-masted schooner bound for New York with only the clothes on his back and one last dollar in his pocket. Forty days later he arrived in a very shabby condition. His clothes had not been changed since the beginning of the trip! But John had no concern about his appearance or other people's opinion of him. When he was finally ordained in Albany in 1836, how he looked on the outside had not the slightest connection with the happiness that was in his heart. He felt as if he were wearing royal purple velvet, for he was a priest at last.

John made his way to Buffalo along the Erie Canal by boat and train. He was impatient to begin his work! But when he arrived, he found a different picture than his hopes had painted. His church was a half-built building without roof or windows. There was no rectory, no school, no welcoming committee. His home was an attic room in an inn with no closet. "Well," he chuckled, "I have no use for one anyhow."

He soon found that the people of the area had little use for Catholics. They threw mud and manure over the walls of the roofless church; often they found their mark as he said Mass.

John realized that the immigrants living in this unfriendly place had even more need of him, so he thanked God for sending him here. He never missed a day of visiting, even during the fierce and bitter Buffalo winters when icy, howling winds chased at his heels as he made his way from house to house. He served not only German families, but Irish, French and Italian as well.

They, in turn, took care of their "little father" and knitted him caps and sweaters to warm him against the cold. But he would pass on the clothing to those who, he felt, needed it more. The women would then scold him for being indifferent to their hours of hard work. "How do you think I like to see the beautiful red cap I knitted for Father on the head of lazy old Fritz who drinks?" muttered one. And John would gently remind her what Christ said about clothing the naked and having two coats in your closet. She would understand, but she would still mutter.

After a few years in Buffalo, John decided that he wanted to belong to a community of priests, so he asked permission to join the Redemptorist order. He became a novice in their seminary in Pittsburgh, where there was a need for German-speaking priests. He was sent to work in New York and Ohio and Virginia, and he went willingly. He wanted to touch as many lives as possible.

John did his work so well he was called back to Pittsburgh and told that he had been chosen to be the new general superior of all the Redemptorists in America. This meant he would be in charge of schools, parishes, convents—everything the Redemptorists did—and of getting the money to run them.

This was not for John! To be superior of men older than himself, to be a businessman, or in charge of running anything—oh no, this was not why he had come to America! He wanted only the hard, simple life of a parish priest.

Then he remembered the day in Paris when he opened that envelope and knew his prayer had been answered. He had vowed that he would be God's man always, doing what God willed. It would seem that now, by God's will and grace, he was to be the new general superior. Very well, then, he would get to work.

And he did. He did his work so well God gave him an even harder job. A bishop was needed in the diocese of Philadelphia, and John was nominated. He was shocked. He was speechless. He went quickly to the bishop who would be leaving and, on his knees and in tears, pleaded not to be considered.

"Can't you tell I'm not right for this job?" he begged. "Look at me! Do I *look* like a bishop? Do I *sound* like a bishop? How many bishops do you know with just one pair of shoes?" His pleas made no difference.

John asked the nuns in the convents, schoolchildren, families in the parishes—everyone—to pray for his special intention (which was, *"Please-God-don't-let-me-be-a-bishop!"*). He even wrote to his superior in Rome, asking him to tell the pope that John was not right for the job.

But nothing worked. God would have his way with John. So he sighed, and accepted. "I *guess* You know best. I had better get to work."

In the remaining nine years of his life, John worked to build more schools and parishes. He founded a teaching order of nuns and brought other orders, such as the Christian Brothers, into the city. And he wrote a German-American catechism in his spare time.

At first people would look at John and think, "He is our bishop?"—just as John knew they would. A visiting archbishop once wrote back in a report to Rome that John was "a little inferior, for the importance of such a distinguished city as Philadelphia, rich, intelligent, full of life and importance, surely merits a bishop of another type. . . ." (You'd think an archbishop would know better than to judge such a holy book by its cover and size.)

And when he died at the age of 49, a pious old lady who came by to pay her last respects commented, "Why, to see that humble creature, you'd never think he was a bishop!"

John, standing tall in heaven, might have replied, "Exactly right, dear lady. I am proof that God can do anything. He can even turn an acorn like me into an oak of a bishop. Isn't it amazing?"

Thomas Aquinas

January 28

Once upon a time there was a little boy named Thomas who asked questions all day long. When he woke he asked why the sun rose in the east, and when he got dressed he asked who invented shoelaces and soap, and when he ate breakfast he asked what raisins looked like before they were raisins and why biscuits rose in the oven and how chickens lay eggs. When his mother finally shooed him outside he asked the gardener why the grass was green, where spiders go in winter and when bees sleep. At night he wanted to know why the sun set in the west, where he went when he slept, and could he please have another glass of water?

But the question he asked most, day and night, was "What is God?"

Thomas' mother, Teodora, had 12 other children to take care of, and his prattle exasperated her thoroughly. He was always underfoot, and since he was a quite large little boy, it could be dangerous for her to be tripping over him constantly.

"Thomas," she would snap, "stop that jabbering and go out and pick off the potato bugs." Or, "Please go next door and borrow a cup of olive oil." Thomas, who was very mild-mannered and obedient, would do what she said. Then he would bounce right back, asking her, "What is God?" Teodora said he was just like a fly hovering about her head on a hot day.

But both Teodora and his father Landolfo knew that Thomas was a "different" child and that God must have a special purpose for him. They didn't know what. At first they thought he was slow-witted, because he didn't talk much or move quickly or get excited about anything. They could not possibly imagine the exciting life that was going on in his brain.

His family were wealthy and respected citizens of the town of Roccasecca. At that time, sons of wealthy nobleman became either knights or priests. Thomas certainly showed no talent for fighting, so his parents decided he would become a monk. At the age of five they sent him off to the nearby Benedictine abbey of Monte Cassino. Maybe the monks could answer his never-ending questions, they hoped.

Teodora and Landolfo also hoped that Thomas would become a learned monk, perhaps even the abbot of the monastery in time. Wouldn't they all be proud of him then! They already had soldiers and a poet in the family and, no doubt, a daughter or two would become nuns—but an abbot, that would be a real feather in their cap!

So off Thomas went to the abbey. He did so well that by the time he was 12 the monks could teach him no more; they sent him to the University of Naples for more study. Thomas loved the city and all the opportunities he had to learn.

One day he went into a Dominican church, knelt down and instant-ly felt a great peace. Something in his heart said, "This is it, Thomas. Here you will find your answers." And the friars welcomed him, little knowing what a very special soul God had directed to them.

After three more years Thomas, who was 20 now, asked the Dominicans if he could join them, and they were as joyful as he in accepting him. They already suspected that within this large body (he stood six feet, six inches tall, with a great square head set on a thick neck) was a mind the likes of which the world had not seen.

So with great pride he put on his rough black and white woolen habit and made ready to go to Rome to study. He was a bit worried about how his mother would take the news. He knew she and the family would be upset, but *upset* wasn't the word. They were *furious*!

In those days, the Dominicans and the Franciscans were not well thought of. They were considered strange, radical dreamers, with neither bed nor roof nor food to give them security.

"This is absolutely unheard of!" said his mother, white with anger. "I will not have my son looking like a beggar and acting like a beggar, going about in sandals and begging for crusts. Oh, what terrible shame has come to us!" Then she fainted and was taken to her room, where she stayed for three days. During that time she planned how she would save Thomas from such a fate.

She called on two of her soldier sons and told them to capture Thomas and bring him home until he came to his senses. So they did. They hid in the bushes along the road and as he walked by, counting the stars, they jumped out, knocked him to the ground and tied him with rope. At first it was quite a struggle because Thomas was very strong. But finally he gave in and held tight to his habit so it wouldn't get ripped in the scuffle.

His family took him to the tower of their castle and kept him prisoner there for a year. His younger sisters brought him books secretly, and he used the days and weeks learning the Scriptures backwards and forwards. Finally, a soft-hearted sister, Marotta (who became a nun much later), made plans with the Dominicans to help Thomas escape.

Somehow they sneaked a huge basket into his room and packed him into it and *somehow*, like Paul, he was pushed through the window and lowered safely to the ground. With the waiting Dominicans he quickly escaped off into the night. (When we get to heaven, I'd like to find out just how Thomas' sisters got him through that tiny tower window!)

He went to Paris and then to the university at Cologne, Germany, to study with one of the finest of the Dominican teachers, St. Albert the Great. Thomas said little but his brain never stopped listening and working. The other students considered him dull because he didn't enjoy arguing or showing off in class. They made fun of him behind his back and called him the Dumb Ox.

Albert just smiled because he knew that someday the joke would be on them. "You may call him a dumb ox," he shook his finger at them, "but some day you will hear his bellowing all over the world."

Soon after Thomas was ordained, he returned to Paris to study, teach, lecture and write about the Christian faith. Students were eager to be in his classes because he set their minds spinning. He did not believe in presenting answers to be learned. Instead, he led his pupils to think for themselves and to find their own answers.

And in all his writings (he wrote over 60 books), he led his

readers to do the same thing—*think* for themselves. He didn't want people to accept the truths about God and his creations just because someone *told* them to. He said that nothing that was true or right could be proven wrong, so they should discuss and reason and use their intelligence. "It is holiness itself, using natural talents to witness to the truth," he said.

The most famous of his books is called the *Summa Theologica*, in which he explained and defended the Christian beliefs. Thomas could never stop asking questions—and then answering them. In this book he answered over 10,000 questions, or objections, which non-Christians had about our faith.

Even greater than his mind was a heart that was unable to love anything, even learning, more than God. The love he had for our Lord spilled over onto everyone he met and they, in turn, soaked up his gentle love like a blotter in the rain. He drew as many into the Church by his warm charm as by the cold brilliance of his mind. He enjoyed nature and art and music and said that "they who abhor pleasures are boorish and ungracious." And to be boorish and ungracious would be to be inconsiderate of others' feelings; our Lord certainly wouldn't want that!

He loved to touch things—pussy willows, cool marble, mud, a kitten's tongue—and said no one could be a good thinker unless he or she was a good toucher. And he had a well-developed funny-bone that enjoyed playfulness; he called it a sin to be sour-faced and "burdensome to others, showing no amusement and acting as a wet blanket."

We know that he was fat—fat enough, it is said, that a hole had to be cut out of the table so he could fit in. We don't know why he was fat. It doesn't seem likely that a saint would steal downstairs at night and eat 10 peanut butter and jelly sandwiches for a snack. Since Thomas didn't talk about it, we don't know if his large size bothered him. It certainly must have been uncomfortable at times. But Thomas may have been absent-minded enough not to notice. He was so busy writing, he probably never bothered to look sideways in a mirror.

One day Thomas stopped writing after he had a vision during Mass. He laid his pen down and said, "I cannot go on. After all I have seen and all that has been revealed to me, all that I have written seems to me like so much rubbish."

He still traveled about teaching, lecturing and writing hymns which we still sing today at Benediction, but he knew that his work in this life was almost done He was on his way to talk to a council in France when he fell ill. His secretary Reginald, who went with him everywhere, was able to help him reach a Benedictine monastery at Fossanuova, and Thomas agreed to stop for a little rest.

The monks were beside themselves with joy that they would be able to care for the great Thomas, who was no longer called the Dumb Ox. They hurried back and forth from the woods carrying armfuls of wood for the fire in his room. The warmth felt good to him, but in his kind way he begged them to stop. They might catch cold going out into those bitter winds.

The young secretary tried to cheer him up. "Can't I please get you something—some cream of asparagus soup, baked custard, *something*?"

Thomas thanked him and thought for a moment. He did remember something he especially liked from his years in Paris. "Ah, a bit of herring would taste so good. I haven't had it in years."

So Reginald ran around trying to find some herring, but to his dismay there were none to be found. A fishmonger passed by just then calling his wares. Reginald stopped him, "Please, sir, would you by some miracle have some herring? My master, Friar Thomas, is quite ill, and he would love a herring."

The fisherman frowned. "Got no herring, but how about a kipper? Kipper would make him chipper!"

"No, kipper won't do. Are you *sure* you have no herring?"

"Well, how about sardines? They taste pretty much like herring. Tell him they're baby herring."

So Reginald, feeling sad that he had failed, bought a basket of sardines. He brought it to Thomas, who opened the lid and sniffed with delight. "What a lovely basket of herring! And I thought I'd never taste them again. Such a nice treat—thank you, Reginald." And when Reginald peeked into the basket, he saw herring indeed—large, silvery, fat herring.

Thomas enjoyed a few bites of the fish and told Reginald to share all the rest with the monks. He knelt down slowly and prayed to the Lord for whom he had taught and written so many years. Thomas asked the Lord to forgive anything he did or said that might have been wrong.

And then he went to heaven, where he would finally find out for himself "What is God?"

Paul Miki & Charles Lwanga

February 5 and June 3

Once upon a time there were two young men who had no more in common than bananas and baseballs. One, Paul Miki, lived 400 years ago in Japan and the other, Charles Lwanga, lived 300 years later in the African country of Uganda. Everything about them was different—the color of their skin, their language, their food— even the way they combed their hair. For fun, Paul flew a kite and played a bamboo flute; Charles speared fish and beat the drums.

Their lives were separated by oceans and mountains and centuries. Yet I would not doubt that right this moment they are the best of friends in heaven, for they have one strong bond: They belong to a special group of saints we call the martyrs.

Now what is so special about being a martyr? Weren't all the saints martyrs in some fashion or another? Didn't they all give up their comforts and their lives to follow Christ? And didn't they all get to heaven sooner or later?

Yes, but the martyrs got there quicker. The dictionary says that a martyr is one who suffers *keenly* for his or her faith, even choosing to die rather than lose it.

Dying is something we'd just as soon not think about. We know we have to do it *sometime*, like cleaning under our bed or getting a booster shot, and we know that death is our bridge from this life to heaven. But we love this life so much, we hope that bridge stays

out of sight. It's like being on a journey and enjoying the journey so much we've forgotten where we're going.

The martyrs knew where they were going. They knew their lives could end quickly and cruelly, usually without warning, simply because they were Christians. They could expect to be torn apart by the lions, thrown into fires, hung from crosses, beheaded, stoned, or thrown off cliffs. It wasn't something you would want to wake up to in the morning. Some of their stories are so gruesome they make us shudder. We'd much rather enjoy the saints who told riddles or moved mountains or made chicken soup and died peacefully in bed at the age of 96.

But the martyrs had absolutely perfect faith that God would get them through the bad moments and would be waiting for them with open arms as they rushed pell-mell across the bridge. How else could they look into the jaws of a ravenous lion with such joy?

These instant saints filled a very special need. Their one blazing moment of courage lit the way for brand-new Christians and for those who may not have heard of Christ at all. The martyrs were seed-saints, Holy Johnny Appleseeds, who shed their blood on soil which needed that nourishment *right then*.

Paul Miki and Charles Lwanga were such seed-saints. Paul was a Japanese Jesuit brother who chose to follow in the footsteps of Francis Xavier, spreading Christ's message in his land. He knew that the missionaries who came across the oceans found his people to be a strange and sometimes confusing race.

The Japanese were most often gentle and courteous. Good manners, they said, is the art of offending no one. Like Bridgid of Ireland, they would give a visitor everything in their desire to please. They had a great love for simplicity and order (Japanese children never had messy bedrooms or left dirty dishes on the table) and nature. A poet could spend years writing about a rose heavy with the morning dew or a chickadee in the lilac bush.

But sometimes they could also kill a servant or enemy or wife just before lunch and sit down to eat without being upset about it. Japan was a land of hard, unforgiving traditions. Like every land, it needed Christ's love to warm its people's hearts so they might see the cruelty of their ways.

When Francis came to Japan in 1549, the rulers welcomed him and the missionaries who were to follow. But 40 years later the Christians led an uncertain life. Their growing power had frightened the rulers, who decided to do away with them. The Christians at once went into hiding, but it was too late for Paul Miki and 25 other Christians who were his friends. They were captured and condemned to die because they refused to deny that they were Christians.

Paul and his companions were quite a mixed bag of would-be saints. It was as if God had handpicked a bouquet of flowers from different fields. There were Jesuit and Franciscan brothers, young altar boys and old men, a doctor, a servant, an artist and a carpenter— each serving God in a different way and all to die for him the same way.

They were taken to Nagasaki to a spot called the Hill of Wheat, where 26 crosses awaited them. A light covering of snow fell softly, a small comfort of beauty which the Japanese would appreciate. Some of their fellow Christians came out of hiding to offer them gifts of food and wine. Even though eating was not on their minds at that moment, the Christians took bits of fish and sips of wine so they would not offend their friends.

As the soldiers fastened them to the crosses, the Christians started to sing. The three altar boys, in their high-pitched voices, burst forth with these words: "Praise the Lord, all ye children!"

And Paul, in what voice he had left, began to preach to his people. He reminded them he was a true Japanese and that he was being killed simply because he was following Christ. "I thank God it is the reason for which I die," he smiled. "I want to say to you again, ask Christ to help you become as happy as I am . . . . I do not hate my persecutors. I forgive them, as he did. I pray God have pity on them and that my blood fall on this Japan and my brothers as a fruitful rain . . . ."

So also did Charles Lwanga, a young black Christian of Uganda, offer his life as a fruitful rain for the faith in his country. He was a member of the Kabaka's royal household and first learned about Christ from another member, Joseph Mukaso, who was in charge of the royal pages.

When Mwanga, who hated all Christians, became the new Kabaka, he was determined that none of his people would ever become one. When Joseph scolded him for murdering a Protestant missionary, Mwanga accused him of being a Christian spy. When Joseph told him he was not a spy but he was indeed a Christian, the enraged ruler put an end to him by removing his head. That very night Charles was baptized.

Charles quickly took over the care of the 21 young pages. He gathered them together and baptized them, for he had a feeling they were not long for this world. "We shall all go to heaven together," he promised them, "so let us think about how wonderful it will be."

The very next morning, Mwanga ordered Charles and the pages to come before him. "Declare, if you dare, that you are Christians!" he roared.

They stood up and quietly and firmly answered, "Yes, we follow Christ the Lord!"

Mwanga sneered and laughed coarsely. "And how long do you remain Christians, now that I know about you?"

"Forever!" they called out together.

"Till death!" added Kizita, who was 13 and the youngest.

"Very well then, go to your God in that place you call heaven, and good riddance to the lot of you! Put them to the fire," he ordered the executioner.

So they went on their way, a chattering, excited band who seemed more to be going to a wedding feast than their own funeral. A missionary priest from France watched as they passed by and later wrote: "I was not allowed to say a word to them and had to content myself with seeing on their faces . . . the happiness and courage of their hearts."

They were bound and thrown into prison, and for seven days they listened to the sounds of carpenters sawing and hammering and whistling. They knew a large wooden platform was being built on which the Christians were to be burned. Finally they were brought out and each one bound in a mat of woven reeds.

"We shall see whether the God you trust will deliver you from the fire!" laughed Mwanga as he held a flame to the dried reeds. The flame took hold and above the war chants of the soldiers and the and the crackling of the huge fire, the sweet voices of the young martyrs could be heard: "You may burn our bodies but you cannot harm our souls! Jesus is Lord!"

May the voices of Paul and Charles and *all* the martyrs rush like a joyous wind at our back, rolling, pushing, wishing us *Godspeed!* as we totter off to meet the lions—or whatever else may lie in wait around the corner.

John Bread-and-Water

Lent

There once was a saint
Who won holy fame
As Blessed John Bread-and-Water
(Since he lived in Spain
He went by the name
Of *Juan pan-y-agua*)

And what did he do,
This little brother?
He lived his life through
On just bread and water.

No butter or jam
To spread on each slab,
No chicken or ham
Or picked meat of crab,

No lemon curd custard
Went onto his bread,
Or sardines in mustard,
Or pimiento cheese spread.

He never knew cream cheese
With olives or dates,

He just smiled and ate
The crumbs on his plate.

And what of the crusts
That sat on his platter?
Whether buckwheat or bran,
It just didn't matter.
(Of one thing we are sure,
It was the bread *du jour*.)

And what else did he do,
Brother John of Navarre?
Did he cobble shoes?
Examine a star?

Did he ring the bells?
Or pot the chives?
Or polish shells?
Or dust archives?

He probably did, all this and much more,
Without any fuss or hint of hauteur,
But just as a plus, for the love of our Lord,
He ate only bread, he drank only water.

And that is why, in a tiny note
In a musty book,
You read of John, who is only known
For what he forsook.

Frances of Rome

March 9

Once upon a time, there was a housewife named Frances who felt her work was so important she kept God waiting until she finished it. If she had windows to wash, she'd ask him to please wait in the parlor while she polished every one. If it were Monday morning and she had laundry to hang out, she'd ask if he'd mind holding the clothespins while she hung it on the line. Even when she was kneeling deep in prayer, if the baby fell out of bed, she would stop her conversation with God and go to the child at once. "Sorry, Lord," she would say, "but you know how it is."

It wasn't that Frances thought so little of our Lord that she put everything else before him. It was because she believed in *first things first,* and what came first to her were her husband Lorenzo and her three children, Battista, Evangelist and Agnes. She knew that being a wife and mother to them was the way God wanted her to give her life for him, so she worked at making a home with as much devotion as a nun decorating the chapel for Easter.

You'd think this would have been easy for Frances; she had everything and everyone at hand to help her. She was both loving and lovable and very pretty besides, with dark brown eyes and dark brown hair piled atop her head like a fat, flat roll. Her husband and his family were wealthy and they all lived in a castle with balconies and gardens and turrets that reached to the sky. She had three cooks and a butler and a gardener; upstairs maids and downstairs maids; and one maid who did nothing but brush her mistress' hair and polish her shoes.

But Frances had wanted none of this. What she had really wished with all her heart was to be a nun and spend her life serving only God. Her wealthy parents would have none of that. She would be doing God's will, they told her, only if she married the young noble-man, Lorenzo, and then everyone would be happy. So she did, and everyone—except Frances—was happy.

Oh, she wasn't *terribly* unhappy, because Lorenzo really did love his young bride (she was only 13) and so did his family. So Frances tucked away her sadness where only God could see it and said, "Very well, Lord, you want me to be a wife? Help me to be the best!"

She bustled about the castle and in a short time began to enjoy her role as mistress of the manor. She learned the first names of all 23 servants and investigated every nook and cranny of her new home. She pulled back the velvet drapes to let the sun shine in and made sure the linen sheets were ironed. She stocked the cellar with wood and wine and apples and the pantry shelves with garbanzo beans and plum jam and Lorenzo's rum tobacco. She was very busy putting *first things first*.

But sometimes, just now and then, when she was alone, she would remember how she had wanted to keep house for our Lord alone and keep *his* shelves stocked high with her good deeds. Then she would sit on a little stool in her closet and weep.

One day her sister-in-law Vannozza found her in such a mood

and was quite upset. Whatever could be wrong with sunny Francesca who was never sad?

Frances loved Vannozza as if she were her real sister, so she wiped her eyes and confided in her. Vannozza burst out laughing. "You too, Francesca? I have wanted to be a nun all my life. Now here we are, brides together in this house! Come on, let's be brave and noble together and make this castle a happy place! Aren't we lucky we have each other?"

They vowed to serve God outside the castle as well, in whatever way they could. They asked their husbands if they might go out each day to help the poor of Rome, and their husbands gave them both money and blessings. Lorenzo kissed Frances as they went out the door with their hampers stuffed full of sausage and olive oil and garlic bread and parsley and tomatoes and little bouquets of marigolds and peppermint sprigs for the children.

"Go where God sends you, my dear," he smiled, "but be home for supper."

So the two young women began their new venture. They put on their plainest clothes and sweetest smiles and went out to make life easier for the needy in the busy city. In a few years, however, when Frances and Lorenzo were blessed with children, it was Vannozza who kept on the work with the poor. Frances stayed home and took care of the babies. She fed them and bathed them and rocked them to sleep and, in between that, she still managed the affairs of the castle.

"A woman such as I must never forget she is a housewife," she said to Vannozza, as they cut out molasses cookies. "Sometimes she must leave God at the altar and find him in her housekeeping." She put down her rolling pin and sighed, "Most of the time I feel like a yo-yo, pulled and spinning in every direction and getting absolutely nowhere." And Vannozza nodded her head, "How true!"

To our Lord, Frances apologized, "What do I have to give you? Just interruptions and distractions, bits and pieces of trying to do your will."

But our Lord understood about those interruptions and sent her a special gift to make her feel better. One morning Frances tiptoed out of bed to say her prayers. It was not yet dawn and a few sleepy stars were still winking. At last she had some time alone with our Lord! No sooner did she kneel down and open her book to morning prayers than Lorenzo called to her to come watch the sunrise. She marked her page and went at once to the window, and together they marveled at the purple sky turning pink, with a few puffs of whipped-cream clouds.

Very well. She had seen the sunrise, now back to her book. She knelt down and took out the marker—and there was a knock at the door. The downstairs maid popped in and bowed. There was a beggar at the kitchen door, would it be all right to give him the leftover liver and onions from the night before? "Of course," Frances said, "and give him the apple dumplings too."

She got back on her knees and opened the book to the same page. Another knock. This time it was the new young cook who couldn't remember whether to put the dill and garlic at the *bottom* of the jar or the top when she made the sour pickles. Frances told her the bottom, and praised her for being smart enough to ask.

The young girl hurried off and before Frances could close the door she heard little Agnes sobbing in the hallway. The boys had snatched her doll with the red hair and thrown it up into the plum tree. Frances hugged her and called to the gardener to rescue the doll. Then she found her sons and set them down to write *I must not tease my sister* 100 times. "And if you do it again," she warned them, "you will go to the cellar and crack one bushel of black walnuts."

Wearily, she closed the door—and then jumped a little with surprise. A magnificent angel bathed in light was writing something in her prayerbook. She came up quietly behind him and peeked over his shoulder. There, in a beautiful gold script, he had written: "Therefore, God has blessed you forever."

These were the very words where Frances had left off each time she had been interrupted. Frances looked at the angel with disbelief. "Why would God bless me when I can't sit still long enough to pray to him?"

"Because you showed your love for him by doing exactly what he wants you to do—loving and taking care of your family."

From that time on for the rest of her days on earth, Frances and her guardian angel were the best of friends. He came to her, it is said, in the form of a little golden-haired boy whom no one else but Frances could see. They visited and walked in the gardens and had tea. He even brought his own cup, which was invisible too.

Then a great plague swept across Italy and soon the streets of Rome were filled with the dying. Frances' happy world grew sad as first Evangelist and then Agnes died. A war broke out and Lorenzo and Battista were carried off as prisoners. Frances and Vannozza

ran out of food and money, so they sold their furs and jewels and silver candlesticks and crystal goblets. When the money from that was gone, they went door to door, begging for food and medicine to help the sick.

Frances thought her family life had come to an end. She was now alone. So she asked the bishop for permission to found an order of women who lived in the world, who made no vows but simply offered themselves to God to serve the poor. And she received it.

Then, out of the blue and to her joy, Lorenzo and Battista were set free and came home. She told Lorenzo about the society she wanted to form and call the Oblates of Mary and asked if he'd mind if she did that and still lived at the castle. "Of course not, my dear," he smiled, "as long as you are home for supper."

For three years Frances lived at home and worked with her Sisters during the day. Then Lorenzo died and Battista married; so Frances left her home of 40 years and went to live with the women of her community. She was so grateful to God that she was able to serve him now as she had wanted since she was a child,

One night when she was visiting Battista and his bride Mobilia, she felt tired. So she said her prayers and went to bed early. She felt a warmth on her face and opened her eyes. The room shone with a golden light, the color of the twilight sun on a winter afternoon.

She sat up and called to her son and his wife, "Goodbye, my loves! My angel has finished his task and holds my hand. I must follow!"

And so she did. But first she must stop by the house, and she asked the angel to wait just a moment by the old plum tree. She opened the door to the kitchen, hung up her apron, swept the floor and put away the broom, watered the geraniums and put down a saucer of milk for the cat. Then she closed the door behind her.

Her house was in order, her work was done. She called to the angel. "I'm ready, let's go!"

And off they went to an eternity of being with God without interruption.

$\mathcal{P}$atrick

March 17

There was once a bishop born of a Roman father and a French mother who became the patron saint of Ireland. The Irish, a people of ready wit, say God must be Irish to play such a joke! Well, that we can't prove. What we do know is that the bishop was God's own gift to Ireland and to all of us.

His name was Patricius, son of Calpornius (the way the Irish form a name, that would make him Patrick McAlpern). We know him best as good St. Patrick, the missionary saint who turned the hearts of the pagan Irish to God. He did it so well that now, 15 centuries later, we find it hard to imagine Ireland as a country where people worshiped tree spirits and the gods of sun and moon and thunder. Today Ireland is known as a country of scholars and saints and people who love words almost as well the Word. And you might say it all happened because Patrick was a lazy boy who couldn't abide school.

We're not sure where Patrick was born. It might have been in Scotland or England, or in a coastal town of Wales. Wherever he lived, it was in much comfort and style. His father was a Roman soldier stationed in England, and the family was quite happy in their life in this new land. Their home was like a Roman villa, with tiled floors and baths and gardens and wall hangings. Patrick enjoyed waking in the morning to the sound of waves hitting the shore and the call of sea gulls to get up, get ready, get to school.

School was the worm in Patrick's apple. He hated to study. When his mother called up at night and asked if he was doing his homework, he would lie and call back, "Yes, mother, I'm almost finished." And then he would continue whittling his slingshot.

One day when the sun was lovely and warm and shone on the water like a handful of scattered diamonds, Patrick decided he couldn't *bear* to sit in a stuffy classroom and learn about the stars or Latin or God. So instead of taking the road to school, he followed the path that led to the shore. He leaped over tree roots and swung from limbs and pretended he was hiding from the fierce Scots or Picts. They would never catch him! Then he ran along the shore, stopping to pick up small white stones for his slingshot.

Then he froze on the spot. A black pirate ship, captained by Niall of the Nine Hostages, swooped into the cove and made a raid on the village. They grabbed every young man and girl they could find—including Patrick—and carried them screaming on board the creaking ship. Then they set sail for Ireland, a land Patrick knew to be filled with wild men and beasts.

When they reached Ireland the captives were sold in the marketplace. The air was filled with the gentle jabbering of an unknown tongue, Gaelic. Patrick, for the first time in his life, was frightened. Oh, how he wished he were back in his classroom! But God had another school in mind for him. He was sold to Milchu, a chieftain who needed a shepherd for his herd of sheep and swine.

For the next six years, Patrick was that shepherd, tending the animals on the slope of a mountain called Slemish. It was a way of life about which he knew nothing, but he got his wits about him and learned quickly. He built himself a hut and kept a fire going day and night to keep the wolves away. He learned the language and made friends with the people, especially the children of Milchu. In the winter he lived in the kitchen and helped make cheese and butter.

Soon he began to love his life and his solitude. Never before had he thought about God as he did now. Like the Old Testament shepherd, David, he let the Lord become his refuge and his joy. "Constantly, I used to pray in the daytime," he wrote. "Love of God increased more and more and my faith grew and my spirit was stirred up . . . . Before the day, I was aroused to prayer, in snow and frost and rain, because the spirit was fervent within."

He thought about his old life very seldom now. Then one night in a dream, he heard a voice telling him to fast and pray, for soon he would be going home. Patrick woke and his heart pounded with excitement. It had been so real! So he did fast and pray, and in a few nights he had another dream. The same voice said, "Go now, Patrick, your ship is ready, *go!*"

So Patrick got up and left in the night, taking nothing with him. He walked along the coast, asking kind villagers for food and a bed for the night. He had traveled almost 200 miles and was nearly exhausted when he saw a ship just about ready to leave, and the voice within said, "Here's your ship, Patrick, run!" And he caught it with the help of a crewman who threw him a rope.

Patrick thought his troubles were over. He was on a ship sailing out of Ireland, away from captivity. He was a free man. He was also a strong, healthy young man of 22 and the crew was glad to have him aboard to help. They put up with his talk of God but didn't really listen to him. That was none of their affair.

Three days out to sea, there was a storm of great violence which tossed them about. Finally the boat ran aground on the shores of France. The crew searched for food and water in vain. The sun beat down upon them and many fainted and fell in little heaps in the sand. The captain, who was still standing, laughed weakly and said to Patrick, "Well, Christian, where is your God now? If he is so high and mighty, why doesn't he take care of us? Doesn't he know we are starving?"

Patrick knelt down and prayed with all his heart, "Please, Lord, send some food. And please don't take too long if you want them to believe."

And, wouldn't you know, at that moment a herd of wild pigs came out of the woods. The sailors were overjoyed. They would not die now, they had food. Patrick went into the woods and found a hollow log stuffed with honey and a small tree covered with little red apples. That night by the light of a fire they had pork chops and applesauce.

Patrick said good-bye to the sailors and went his own way. Again, we are not sure, but we think he went to visit his mother's brother, St. Martin of Tours, and then to an island off southern France where he lived in a monastery and studied to be a priest. One night after he was ordained, he again heard a voice in his dream—the same voice he had heard many years ago in Ireland.

It was his guardian angel speaking, showing him an armful of letters. On the top one were the words, *The voice of the Irish*. As Patrick began to read, he heard the sweet, plaintive lilt of Gaelic spoken by the people he knew, calling to him. "We beg you, holy boy, to come and walk once more among us."

Patrick awoke and knew without a doubt that his life now had a definite mission. He was to return to the land where he was once held captive and bring the Irish to the true faith.

When he was in his 40's and a bishop, Patrick finally set sail for Ireland with a band of young and zealous missionaries. As soon as he set foot on shore he began to preach. The pagans, at first afraid, caught the saint's fervor and were converted. Never were people so ready to hear what Christ had to say!

They told Patrick that there would be a gathering of the chieftains and Druid priests at Tara, the castle of the High King Laoghire, to celebrate the birthday of the new year. Here the fire for the new year would be lighted by the Druid priests. On the day before, all the old fires were to be put out and none relighted until the flames from the new one could be seen from Tara.

Now the evening of their festival was also the eve of Easter. Patrick knew that one thing the chieftains respected was a show of courage, and he was not one to be timid. He had been through enough adventures and hardships to make him tough and clever. He was also bold, stubborn and hot-tempered, so if anyone said to him, "You can't build a fire tonight," you can imagine what his answer would be.

So Patrick and his band went up to the top of the Hill of Slade, directly across from Tara, and there "kindled a fire in the nostrils of King Laoghire." The Druids were aghast when they saw the flames of the Christians' Easter fire licking the sky. They hurried to the king and told him he must kill the fire *and* Patrick immediately, "for this fire will blaze forever in our land if it is not put out at once."

The king gave orders to the warriors and priests to storm the Hill of Slade. Up they climbed, wheezing and grunting under the burden of buckets of water, to put out the worrisome fire. But try as they might, even stamping on it and dousing it with earth and sand, the fire would not go out. Patrick and his men knelt down and sang, "Let God arise and let his enemies be scattered!"

The king, who was a very smart man, wondered to himself what manner of man this Patrick was, who would kneel down and sing while his enemies circled about him. And what kind of fire would not go out? He admired Patrick's bravery and ordered him to come to his court the next morning and tell him about this new faith.

The Druid priests were upset and angry. They were quite satisfied with the tree gods and wood nymphs and feared they would be destroyed by Patrick's God. They decided to kill Patrick themselves. The next morning as Patrick and his men made their way to Tara, the Druids hid in ambush along the road. As the singing of the men grew closer, they made ready their spears and clubs. Then they sprang from the bushes—and what did they see?

A doe leading 20 fawns! The Druids fled, fearing a magic spell would be cast upon them if they touched the animals. The song which the deer sang (they were, of course, Patrick and his band) has come down to us as "St. Patrick's Breastplate," a song filled with the saint's trust that if he cast his cares upon the Lord, the Lord would sustain him:

> *I arise today,*
> *God's strength guiding me,*
> *God's might sustaining me,*
> *God's wisdom directing me,*
> *God's eye looking before me,*
> *God's ear listening to me,*
> *God's word speaking for me,*
> *God's hand protecting me,*
> *The way of God stretching out before me,*
> *The shield of God as my shelter . . . .*

King Laoghire never became a Christian, but his queen and the two princesses wanted to become Christians. They could understand everything, they said, except the Blessed Trinity. How could there be three people in one, they asked Patrick?

He reached down and, from the abundance of shamrocks growing underfoot, picked one. "Do you see this little plant?" he asked them. "It is one plant, one stem, but it has three leaves. Three leaves on one stem. And that is the way with the Trinity. God is the stem, the three leaves are the Father, the Son and the Holy Spirit. Now do you understand?" They did, and became Christians on the spot.

From that day on, Patrick never sat still a moment. He traveled the green meadows and hills of Ireland tirelessly for 30 years. He was never deterred by cold or hunger or thirst. He sometimes slept on bare stone with a wet cloak about him, a rock for his pillow. It seemed as if God's light did surround and protect him, for he almost single-handedly changed the hearts of the Irish with Christ's truth. And it was done without bloodshed.

There was just one instance of injury, an accident for which Patrick was very sorry. When he was baptizing King Angus of Cashel, he brought the spike of his bishop's staff down sharply, like an exclamation point, to emphasize a point in his sermon. The staff went right through the king's big toe.

The king said nothing although his eyebrows shot up quickly and his face turned a shade pale. When Patrick found out what he had done, he was all sympathy and bound up the bloody toe himself.

"Why didn't you tell me?" he asked the king.

"I thought it was part of the ceremony," the king answered bravely.

Patrick laughed, "You may have to give up some things to be a Christian, but not your *toe!*"

Patrick baptized 120,000 souls by his own hand, founded 700 churches, ordained 5,000 priests and 370 bishops. Some say he was able to accomplish so much because he was such a practical saint and traveled equipped for everything. The Boy Scouts should have him as their special saint, they add, because he certainly knew how to *be prepared*. He would come with a household of 12 clerics (native Irish boys who were going to become priests), an assistant bishop, a chaplain, a judge for legal matters, a strong man, bell-ringers, blacksmiths, cooks, brewers, gardeners, bricklayers, cowherds, carpenters, masons, artists, seamstresses and, of course, a poet and a musician.

After he had baptized the people of a village, Patrick would look for a spot he felt was right for their church. His household would come to a halt and in a clatter of pots and hammers and bells and harps set to work digging the foundation. Blacksmiths forged nails and door-hinges. Artists and coppersmiths gave beauty to the altar and vessels while seamstresses embroidered the linens. When the church was ready for its first celebration of Mass, Patrick would give it a name and leave the new parish in the hands of a young priest. Then the household would travel on and do the same thing in another spot the next day.

This is how Patrick spent his life. In 30 years, all of Ireland became Christian—which amazed even Patrick. He was humble enough to know that only God, working through him, could do this. He wished—oh, how he wished!—that he had not been such a lazy student. If he were a scholar, he thought, he could have done even greater things.

Nonetheless, God used him for extraordinary work. It could be that God knew he could depend upon Patrick, through thick and thin, hill and bog. Patrick was reliable, he was steadfast.

If you have ever read Hans Christian Andersen's story, *The Steadfast Tin Soldier*, you may recognize some of his qualities in Patrick. He too was brave, single-minded and absolutely certain that one day he would be united with his one true Love. Every morning he prayed that God would keep him steadfast:

> *May the strength of God guide me this day,*
> *and may his power preserve me.*
> *May the wisdom of God instruct me,*

the ear of God hear me,
the Word of God give sweetness to my speech,
the hand of God defend me.
And may I follow the way of God!

Patrick is the saint for all who would stand fast and hold tight to God's Word, no matter what. Patrick will help us to overcome the pirates and Druids and shipwrecks of our own lives with no trouble at all.

And if your name happens to be Patrick McAlpern, just think what he will do for *you*!

Joseph

March 19

Joseph, they say,
Was quiet and good,
He prayed all the while
He whittled his wood.

He was gentle and just
And quite ordinary,
This carpenter who married
The young virgin Mary.

'Twould be simple, he thought,
Their way of life,
In Bethlehem's nest
As husband and wife.

This was all he asked,
All he'd expect,
But God had plans for Joseph
He didn't suspect.

He whispered them to Gabriel,
Who mentioned them to Mary,
Who carried the secret
Like a pit in a cherry.

But no one told Joseph,
Who was left in the dark,
Fumbling for the answer
To a stubborn question mark.

Then in a dream an angel
Said nothing was amiss—
The Son that Mary carried
Was simply God's, not his.

"How can this be?"
He puzzledly exclaimed,
The angel only shrugged,
"Because God so proclaimed!"

Surely, there were others
Of the House of David's tree,
Who could serve a royal child
More appropriately!

The angel reassured him
In no uncertain voice:
"Joseph, you are handpicked,
You're the Father's choice!"

So he went about his work,
This ordinary man,
Hammering his life
Into the Master's plan.

And Mary and Jesus
And himself, all three,
Were a family as special
As the Blessed Trinity.

He went to the fields
To show Jesus how
To cast the seeds
And work the plow

And prune the vines
And budge the boulder
And find the sheep
Lost in the alder

And swing the axe
With one good stroke
To fell the cedar,
Pine and oak.

He showed his Son
That a house must be built
On solid rock
And not on silt.

They worked in the shop
And planed the beams
And made a wagon
And joined the seams

And fashioned wheels
And baskets and benches,
All with a saw
And nails and wrenches.

They hummed and prayed
And measured and whistled,
While wood chips curled
Under their chisels,

Then went home weary
When work was done
To Mary and chowder
And cinnamon buns.

The years flew by
As he stood in the wings,
Coaching his Son
For greater things.

Of where he died,
We have no notion,
Or whether he lies
In hillock or ocean,

But they say on Good Friday
When Jesus died,
Joseph ascended
To the Other Side.

God hugged him tight
As a long-lost brother,
Rather it was more
One Father to another.

Despite all this, he
Would ever find it odd
That a man with shavings in his beard
Should raise the Son of God.

Catherine of Siena

April 29

There was once a young woman who spoke with such wisdom everyone stopped to listen. Kings and soldiers and princes and popes waited for her every word. And she not only spoke, she sent letters by the buckets, hundreds and hundreds filled with strong advice sweetly offered. They were so powerful whoever read them would slap the table, jump up and say, "Yes, yes, she's right, and by God's grace, I shall do it!"

Her name was Catherine of Siena. She was the 24th child and youngest daughter of Jacopo and Lapa Benincasa, who were wool dyers in the town of Siena in Italy. Can you imagine being the youngest child in a family of that size? Catherine liked to be alone and learned very early to find her own amusement. What she liked to do best was to close the door to the tiny room at the top of the stairs and sit on the red brick floor, as if it were an enchanted island, and dream and pray.

The next best thing was to climb up and down the stairs leading to her room, kneeling on each stair as she said a Hail Mary. Her mother didn't mind at all. At least it kept her out of mischief. "But be careful coming down, little one. I have enough problems without your banging your head!"

Sometimes her older brother Stephen took her out to play hopscotch or count dandelions or visit the store where they sold lemon ices. One evening just before supper, they were outside watching the sunset over the Church of St. Dominic on top of the hill. The sky was splashed with gold and scarlet and pink. As Catherine soaked in the beauty to save in her memory, she saw more than brilliant colors.

Catherine saw our Lord on his throne, surrounded by his disciples Peter, Paul and John, all shining and joyous in splendid robes. Jesus stretched out his hand and blessed the little girl. Catherine stood motionless, as if she had turned to stone. Stephen shook her roughly. He was very frightened. Catherine was not breathing, yet she *couldn't* be dead standing up. Oh, what would their mother say! He shook her again, urgently.

She gave a start and quickly looked back at the sky. The vision was gone. She began to cry and sob and beat on Stephen angrily. "Why did you do that? Now he's gone. Oh, if you had seen what I saw, you wouldn't have shaken me!"

Poor Stephen! He had seen nothing and thought Catherine had been out in the sun too long.

But Catherine knew what she had seen was real. Jesus had come to her and invited her to be his. From that moment, she vowed to belong to Christ alone. Everything she did would be at his bidding. This was a secret between Catherine and our Lord for the next six years. No one suspected. She was such a laughing child, running here and there like a golden bird; no one believed she ever had a serious thought in her sunny blond head. Everyone called her Joy, because that is what she was.

When she was 12, her mother brushed out her golden hair and

said soon they would be looking for the right husband for their little girl. Catherine jumped up and said, "No, Mother, I will marry no one. I have already promised myself to Jesus."

Now Jacopo and Lapa were very good people. They were generous and loving in the care of their 24 blessings from God, but they would not hear of such nonsense from a child! What did she know of life or God or *anything*? They asked a priest to come and talk with her. By the time he was through, he was convinced she was right. He whispered to her as he left, "If you are serious, cut off your hair."

Now a young woman's hair in those days was truly her crowning glory. The longer her hair, the more beautiful she was considered. If, by some mishap, it was cut off, no one would want to marry her. So Catherine grabbed her scissors and chopped and chopped until she looked ghastly.

Her parents were furious. How dare she ruin their plans! To bring her to her senses, they dismissed all the servants and turned the work of the house over to Catherine. So she cooked and swept and washed and hung out laundry for 26 people. She did it without sulking or talking back. After all, she thought, the martyrs had worse things to bear than peeling potatoes for a large family.

They took away her tiny room so she would have no more time for her silly dreaming. When she sniffled a little about this to our Lord, he told her that she must turn in to the cell of her heart, where she would always find him. He reminded her that he was always with her, strengthening her. She didn't need her room for their visits.

One day, when she was scraping the burnt crust off the roast pan with her finger nail, her father walked in and saw a white dove nestled on her shoulder, his soft wing brushing her hair. By God's grace, his mind was opened and he knew the dove was the Holy Spirit. He put his arms around his little girl and promised she would never have to marry anyone on this earth.

"Let her serve her Bridegroom in complete freedom," he told his wife. "We could never obtain so honorable a marriage for her. Instead of a mortal man, we have been given the immortal God-made-man!"

For the next three years, Catherine lived in her little room, going out only for Mass at the convent church. She prayed, mostly, and visited with our Lord. Then God gave her the gift of reading. She didn't learn to read as we do, starting with the alphabet. She just sat down one day, opened a page of the Psalms and rattled it off as if she had written it herself. Now she could read her prayers as well as think them.

One night Jesus came and told her it was a very special visit. He put a gold ring on her finger, which meant she was truly his forever. She promised him, with tears in her eyes, "As the fish arise in the sea, so thou art in me and I am in Thee."

And now, our Lord said, it was time for Catherine to go out and serve him in the sick and poor so they might come to him. Catherine said she'd rather not. She was afraid of the world; she had been away from it so long. And if she were too busy with the world outside, she would be separated from him.

"Catherine," said our Lord, "you know that I have given you two commandments, to love me and to love your neighbor. I ask that you walk not on one but two feet and fly to heaven on two wings."

So right then and there, she told him that her trust in him was stronger than her fear of what awaited her in the world. She combed her hair (which had grown back), straightened her apron and went down to dinner. Everyone was so surprised they could hardly eat. They all talked at once and Catherine asked would someone please pass the lima beans, and it was just like old times, her mother sighed wistfully.

Catherine was 18 now, old enough to become a member of the Dominican Third Order. Even though she was a nun, she still lived at home instead of in a community.

Catherine took her job working with the sick in earnest. She worked at the leper hospital with such love and tenderness that no one ever knew that she couldn't stand sickness and dirt and the unpleasant smells that went with both. She had a passion for clean rooms with clean white curtains and fresh air blowing in the windows, and yet she worked in windowless wards filled with unbathed bodies and soiled sheets as if she were strolling through a bower of honeysuckle.

She took care of the most abandoned and unpleasant patients. At first they resented her because she was pretty, healthy, young—all the things they were not. They blamed God for all their woes and sometimes cursed him. But Catherine ignored this. She looked for the good in everyone and she usually found it. Under the bad temper, greed and just plain meanness, she saw our Lord. And as she washed and soothed and fed grumpy old ladies, she would ask him to heal and touch their hearts as well as their bodies.

There was an old woman named Cecca who was as mean as she

was sick. Meaner! Nobody went near her. Nothing could please her. The soup was too hot, the eggs were too hard, the water too soapy, her braids too tight, and would somebody *please* cut her toenails?

She made fun of Catherine to the others and called her an old maid. "There's nothing else for her to do but take care of us since she couldn't catch a husband. She ought to be glad we give her something to do!"

Catherine let the meanness roll off her heart like butter off a hot griddle. But sometimes, when she wished they would be just a little nicer, our Lord would say to her, "Catherine, I have two crowns, one of gold and one of thorns. Which would you rather have in this life? I will save the other for eternity."

She chose the crown of thorns. After all, if our Lord could die for his enemies, she could bear with Cecca!

One morning Catherine went to the hospital and, as she always did, bathed Cecca's bleeding fingers and bandaged them. Cecca began to screw up her face into a black look. But then her eyes widened. She covered her face with her stumps of hands and began weeping—for when she had looked at Catherine, she had seen instead the face of the Lord.

"Forgive me," she begged the young woman. "I am a cranky old woman who has forgotten how to say thank you. Never again shall I forget!" And she didn't.

Besides nursing the sick, Catherine buried the dead, visited prisoners and became Siena's best peacemaker. Her ability to patch up fights and find the best solutions became so well-known that people talked of her in Florence and Naples and Rome. Her secret was in her complete trust in God to advise and counsel her. She would listen most carefully to both sides of a story and then listen to what God said to her. Then she would tell straight out, without fear, what must be done to set a life or a country in order.

Very often, she sent letters (over 400 of them). Since she had never learned to write, she dictated them to her secretaries. She had three young noblemen who were part of a band of people who followed her everywhere. These poets, artists and scholars were called the *Caterinati*. They rarely left her side and were like daily newspapers, reporting her latest sayings and good deeds. They called her Mama and indeed, she treated them like her children.

She treated everyone like a loving Italian mama, one who is used to being obeyed. She coaxed and scolded and teased and embraced and, of course, gave orders. But she did it so charmingly, especially in her letters, few could resist her suggestions. She wrote to kings and princes and priests and popes with advice on how to bring about peace in their country and in the Church.

At that time, there were always disagreements popping up over something, and God's Word could barely be heard above the clamor of war cries and the clattering hooves of charging horses. But before there could be any peace, Catherine knew, the pope (who was then living in Avignon in France) must come home to Rome, where the head of the Church should be.

She wrote to Pope Gregory with the sweetness of a mother and the force of an archangel. She called him her "sweet babbo" and sent him candied orange peel in a tea tin for a Christmas present with a note that read, "Beyond the first bitter taste you will find sweetness,

as one finds sweetness in the will of the Lord." Then she added that it was the Lord's will that he return to Rome. And he did.

When that pope died, she wrote the new one, Pope Urban, and asked if she might come to Rome to live. He said, "Yes, my daughter, we need you!" He told the cardinals and princes and other important people to listen to the "little woman," *picco donzella*, who had the spiritual wisdom to save the Church.

Catherine went on preaching and teaching with her letters, and when she was 33, she died. In her short life, she had grown from a timid girl who did not want to leave her little room to a fearless advisor to the popes and a Doctor of the Church, as honored as Thomas Aquinas. On the evening that she died, she looked at the sky and caught her breath. It was a wild sky of molten gold and scarlet and rose streaked with purple. It was a sky the like of which she had not seen since she was six years old.

And there in the center of the glorious color was the vision of her youth—Jesus with John and Paul and Peter around him and Mary smiling over them all!

Our Lord reached out his hand, and Catherine hurried to grasp it. She would not lose the vision this time, for now she was part of it.

Our Lady of Czestochowa

Chess-ta-ko-va

May

The stories of our Lady's appearances are so full of awe and wonder they make you catch your breath. The very *thought* of seeing Mary as you go about your chores, taking out the trash or walking the dog or digging potatoes seems unbelievable. And yet, she comes, to saints and sinners and ordinary folk somewhere in between, in form and dress as different as the people she visits, so that everyone will find in her something familiar and well-loved, whether it be in Japan or Africa or Ireland.

But the story of Our Lady of Czestochowa is different. You would think when she came to this town in Poland, she would have been pink-cheeked, blue-eyed and blonde, dressed in bright, gaily embroidered peasant costume with her head wreathed in flowers and ribbons. Instead, she came as the Black Madonna, an image many believe reflects Mary as she actually was.

According to popular belief and old writings, Saint Luke painted a picture of our Lady and the child Jesus when he visited Mary at the home of Saint John, where she lived after Jesus died. As they sat and talked of this and that, Luke, who was an artist as well as a doctor and writer, painted Mary's image on the top of a small table of cypress wood which Jesus had made for her when he was a child. When Mary had moved in with John this was one of the few belongings she brought with her.

101

Saint Sixtus of Siena writes, "Saint Luke . . . with brush and paints made a portrait of the Blessed Mother," and a Roman writer, Nicefar, adds "The portrait of the Blessed Mother Saint Luke painted with his own hands while she was still alive. She saw the painting and impressed into it the pleasing expression of her countenance."

What did Mary look like? Her skin was naturally dark since she lived in the Middle East. Saint Epifanius writes that "her complexion was that of wheat . . . eyes tinted with brown and olive-colored pupils . . . . Her nose was elongated, her blossoming lips full of expression. Her manner . . . was simple and understandable to all."

After Mary died, the painting began a life of adventure and narrow escapes from destruction. During the persecutions of Christians in Jerusalem, it was passed from one caretaker to another, stored secretly in caves or catacombs, always one step ahead of its pursuers. What stories this painting could tell, if it had the gift!

In the year 326, Saint Helena, mother of the Emperor Constantine, decided to travel to Jerusalem to find Christ's cross and this painting she had heard about. After a long search, she found the painting and brought it back to her son, who built a church for it next to his palace.

For the next five hundred years, the painting stayed at the court in Constantinople. Then, when Christianity began to spread to Bulgaria and Russia and Poland and Hungary, and when the emperor's daughters married into the royal families of these countries, the painting went with them as part of their dowry.

By 1382, during the reign of Prince Ladislaus of Poland, the painting had found its home in the chapel of Belz castle. During an attack by Tartar warriors (savage Mongolian tribes that regularly invaded Poland), one of the soldiers climbed through the chapel window and struck the painting with his sword, making a scar on our Lady's neck.

Fearing it might be destroyed, the prince decided to smuggle it into his birthplace in Upper Silesia. By nightfall he had reached the town of Czestochowa. Too tired to go on, he hid the painting in a small wooden church nearby. In the morning he carried it back to the horse-drawn wagon and bade the horses be on their way and *quickly*.

But the horses refused to move. The prince desperately prayed for guidance. What did Mary want him to do with the portrait? Nothing happened—no voices, no heavenly direction. He was left on his own, so he went to sleep.

Then, in a dream, Mary spoke to him. She wanted her picture left right there in Czestochowa, on Jasna Gora, the "Bright Hill." The prince believed that the dream was real and brought the portrait back into the wooden church. Here it stayed until he built a new shrine, which he dedicated to Our Lady of Czestochowa.

It has been almost seven centuries since the painting came to Czestochowa. Only once did it leave, when it was stolen in another invasion, this time by Hussite (Czech) soldiers. It was thrown with other valuables taken from the monastery into a wagon drawn by horses. Once again the horses refused to move, even when the drivers whipped them.

Finally, the soldiers threw the portrait onto the ground, and one of them slashed our Lady's face with his sword, leaving two scars.

When he raised his sword to cut it a third time, a bolt of lightning killed him. The other soldiers, terrified, fled the scene.

The monks who took care of the monastery found the scarred and mud-splattered picture and looked in vain for water to clean it. They prayed to our Lady for help and at once a spring of clear water gushed out of nowhere. They joyfully cleaned the picture and returned it to its rightful place in Czestochowa. From that day to this, the spring bubbles with what many claim to be healing water.

Today, seven centuries later, pilgrims still come to pray at the shrine of our Lady at Jasna Gora. She has become the particular, passionate devotion of the Polish people. All Poles, in and out of Poland, have always had a deep love for the Mother of God. The fact that she chose Poland as the guardian of her priceless image is a source of great pride to them.

This brave country's history is one of never-ending persecution by invaders—Russians, Germans, Turks, Swedes, Czechs, Austrians—who have captured it and divided it up but never conquered it. The Poles give Mary the credit for their survival and victory.

She has granted many miracles *off* the battlefield as well. All seem fantastic; all are documented. Many of the stories have been painted as frescoes on the ceiling of the shrine, stories of miraculous healings, of children dead and cold in their coffins brought back to pink-skin health and laughter, of victims burned at the stake emerging unscathed.

There are tales of our Lady's answering urgent prayers from miner's trapped in a collapsed shaft, of travelers drowning when their boats were torn apart in wild storms, of prisoners about to be hanged or brought before a firing squad, all of whom saw a vision of our Lady comforting them before they were rescued.

One story tells of a well-known judge who died. On the day of his funeral, as his family and friends waited sadly at the grave, the pallbearers raised the casket up onto their shoulders. Suddenly the judge sat upright in the coffin. As you can imagine, there was a lot of screaming and confusion. People thought they were seeing a ghost, but *no*, they discovered he was very much alive. When the noise died down, the judge said, "When I was dying and could not speak, I begged the Madonna to restore my life so I could come back and confess my sins and do penance for them." Then everyone went back to the house to the lunch that had been prepared for the mourners but now was turned into a welcome-home celebration.

And then there was Feliks, a soldier who had been kidnapped by the Turks and imprisoned for refusing to worship their God. He sat in the dark dungeon, arms and legs bound in chains, glumly wondering if this was the end of the road for him. To die was bad enough, but to die away from Poland was worse.

Suddenly he was startled by a light bright as the noonday sun. He smelled roses. Then he saw our Lady with two angels bearing torches on either side of her. She said gently, "Feliks, my son, come visit me at my home on Jasna Gora. I will see you there!"

Immediately the chains fell from his limbs with a loud clank, which he thought would wake the world. But the guards slept on, and he walked right past them. He went out into the street and still nobody stopped him. He wandered unnoticed through Turkey until he reached his homeland. He went to our Lady's shrine as she had asked and told everyone who would listen what had happened.

These stories show Mary as a tenderhearted mother who cannot say no to her children, no matter how whiny or foolish or unruly they may be. She always says, "I'll see what I can do"—and then some. All she asks in return is that we come visit her home sometime.

"Home" can be as far away as Jasna Gora or Knock or Guadalupe; it can be as near as your school chapel or a small country church or a large cathedral. Wherever Mary is, a mother will listen to you.

More Saints Budding Everywhere

Spring/Summer

A Litany for the Garden

When ladybugs bloom
On the kitchen sill,
And bears come out
In the April chill,

The time has come
We know in our marrow
To go and fetch
The rusty wheelbarrow

And pile it high
With garden needs:
With tools and twine
And stakes and seeds,
And leaves and lime
To quell the weeds.

But even before
We rake the stones
We call on the saints
To shake their bones.

They come on the run,
This heavenly crew,
To bless the earth
With holy dew.

O saintly ones
With thumbs of green!
Look with love
On the lima bean.

Protect the pea
And the Chantenay carrot
From slugs and rot
And the mealy-mouthed maggot!

Isidore, I implore
Your kind guarantee
To hold off the hoar,
Bring on the bee,

Coax the wind
And sun and heat

To swell the grains
Of oat and wheat.

Fiacre, please guide
My uncertain hoe
From zigzag ditch
To respectable row.

St. Barnaby, kindly
Blow the whistle
On advancing columns
Of unruly thistle.

And Blase, please tame
Its cousin teasel.
Likewise, dear Martin,
The nightstalking weasel.

Golden girl Clare
Will shower the sun,
And when we need rain,
Odo's the one.

Laughing Bridget's
The saint with the power
To fling free the carpet
Of dandelion flower.

If you would plant flax,
Unsure as to how,

Call upon Stanislaus,
Who lived in Cracow.

There's Lawrence for grapes,
And Botulf for turnips,
Margaret for poppies—
But who, Lord, for parsnips?

St. Philbert, of course,
Is for nuts of all sorts.

There is no end
Of this loving bunch
Who till the plot
For our free lunch.

You'd think the garden
Was a soul
Which they must guard
From moth and mole,

And mice who chew.
If the soil be sour,
No matter. They just smile
And pray and work by the hour,

Weeding and mulching
And warming by hand
This unlikely spot
Of promised land.

Note: Most of the saints mentioned in this "Litany of the Garden" are celebrated in the course of spring and summer: Stanislaus (April 11), Isidore the Farmer (May 15), Bridget (July 23), Lawrence (August 10) and Clare (August 11). And Botulf (June 17), Odo of Canterbury (July 3), Philbert (actually, Philibert, August 20), Fiacre (September 1) and Margaret of Hungary (June 10), while not included in the current Roman Calendar, have been traditionally celebrated in this season. Blase (February 3) and Martin de Porres (November 3) are the exceptions.

Paul the Apostle

June 29

When the Church was very new, there was a man named Saul who did his best to make the lives of Christians miserable. He was a Jew, a proud and powerful Pharisee, who believed only in the law of Moses. He needed only to hear a whisper of a *possibility* that a Christian was nearby and he would erupt like a just-lit firecracker.

He dug and prodded and sniffed and snorted, like a dog determined to find a buried bone, until he unearthed the doomed believers. Then in an explosion of curses and threats, he sent them on their way to heaven. It is no wonder that Saul the Pharisee became known as the Passionate Persecutor of the People of God.

If Christian mothers had told stories about him to their children, he probably would have sounded as frightful as the giant in *Jack the Giant Killer*, thundering: "Fee, fi, fo, fum, I smell the blood of a Christian-son!" (Or daughter.)

But instead of telling stories, they were busy warning them to beware of a stranger riding a white horse—one who was bald and had fierce blue eyes, a big nose and thick black eyebrows that met together across his forehead. He was also bowlegged, but since he was most often on his horse chasing Christians, hardly anyone noticed.

What he didn't have in looks, Saul made up in spirit and determination. There was no doubt in his mind that whatever he thought, said, or did was absolutely right. He never looked at a problem from

two sides and said *maybe*, or *perhaps* he *could* be wrong. He was what you'd call a fanatic, a person who is wildly positive that he is right and positively wild in his way of proving it.

And on top of that, he was impulsive. And he was touchy as a grouchy porcupine, ready to shoot his quills if anyone disturbed him. His poor parents, they had such a handful! Their hearts must have ached wondering what would ever happen to their headstrong, willful son.

Well, one day about five years after Jesus' death, Saul was ready to shoot off his quills again. He had decided to go up to Damascus to round up those trouble-making Christians and bring back as many as he could find to Jerusalem. So, with a few of his Pharisee friends, Saul galloped off into the sunrise on a journey that would turn his whole world inside out and upside down.

They were clattering along—and then it happened. There was a sudden blinding flash of light, like a lightning bolt that shot across the sky and stayed there. Saul's horse bucked and quivered and whinnied and threw his master to the ground. As he lay there, stunned, a voice came out of the heavens, very deep and very clear: "Saul, *Saul*, do you hear me? Why are you doing this to me?"

Saul was startled but not frightened. He answered this question with another question.

"Who are you, Lord?"

And the voice said, "I am Jesus, whom you persecute."

Now Saul was frightened. All the terrible things he had done to Christians, all the hatred he had simmering inside against them— what if it had all been wrong? What if it were possible that they *were* the true believers? In that case, he reasoned quickly, it was only fair that God kill him in return. He lay there trembling, waiting for the flash that would end it all.

But there was only this brilliance and the waiting silence. Saul could not stand waiting. He dared to call out in a faint voice, "Lord, what will you have me to do?"

The Lord told him to keep on the road to Damascus and, when he arrived there, to go to the house of a man named Judas. Then he said that Saul should join the Christians instead of trying to kill them. He wanted Saul to become a Christian!

Saul almost laughed out loud at such a ridiculous idea. Saul the Persecutor, become one of those crazy fools for Christ? But he couldn't even manage a chuckle because he felt strangely excited about it. It seemed so right. He didn't know it then but God had given him his gift of grace. Saul didn't want it, he didn't deserve it, but he *had* it.

Saul thanked God for this second chance and told him he would use all his zeal and energy to work with this grace. He would love and follow Christ as boldly as he had hunted him before. He would be joyful and fearless in telling the world about Christ, no matter where the road and God's will took him.

He pulled himself up and suddenly the brilliance was gone. The voice was gone. The sun had gone too. Everything was black. In a panic, he groped for his horse but could not find him.

"I am blind!" he cried out. Was this to be his punishment for being so cruel? Would he have to work for the Lord without being able to see?

His friends led him to the house of Judas when they got to

Damascus. There he stayed for three days, neither eating nor drinking nor seeing. Now there was a Christian named Ananias who also lived in Damascus, and on the night that Saul came to Judas' house, Christ appeared to Ananias in a dream.

He told him to go to Saul and tell him to be baptized. At that, Ananias woke and thought he had had a nightmare. He knew about Saul, the Christian-killer. The Lord couldn't possibly want Ananias to visit *him*.

He went back to sleep and the dream came back stronger. Jesus added, "Go, Ananias, for this man will carry my name before Gentiles and kings and the children of Israel, and I will show him how much he has to suffer for my name."

At the same time Ananias had his dream, Saul had one too. He saw a man he did not know enter his room and lay his hands upon his eyes and he could see again. He woke and was still lying in his bed thinking about the dream when Ananias came into his room.

Ananias stood by Saul's bed and laid his trembling hands upon Saul's eyes. "Brother Saul," he said, "I have been sent by the same Lord Jesus who appeared to you on the road—that you may receive your sight and be filled with the Holy Spirit."

Immediately great flakes like scales fell from Saul's eyes and he looked with joy upon Ananias. Yes, he was the man in his dream. Saul embraced him.

Ananias said, "The God of our fathers has chosen you to be a witness to all peoples of what you have seen and heard. Why do you tarry? Hurry, arise! Be baptized and washed from your sins, calling on the name of the Lord!"

Saul wasted not a moment. He jumped up, was baptized, and ate a hearty breakfast to celebrate the lifting of darkness from his eyes and his soul.

Then he thought that as long as he was going to have a new life, he would want a new name, and he chose Paul. He immediately went to the synagogue and introduced himself as Paul-who-was-once-Saul and began to preach and praise the Lord he had once hated. Everyone—Jew, Christian, Gentile—was speechless.

Before they had time to make any sense of this, Paul had left Damascus. He went to the desert of Arabia, where he spent the next three years praying and thinking. He wanted to learn about himself and what his special work for the Lord was to be. When he felt he knew, he came back to Damascus, but he was not received with joy.

No one was glad to see him. The disciples were still suspicious of him and didn't trust him. The Pharisees were furious with him for joining the Christians. But Paul paid them no mind and went on preaching with enthusiasm. Gradually the Christians threw away their doubts and accepted him as their brother. He called himself the "13th apostle." (We're so used to thinking of him as Paul the Apostle, it's a small surprise to realize he wasn't one of the original 12.)

Paul was so successful in turning hearts to God that the Pharisees decided the only way to stop him was to kill him. Some disciples overheard the whispered plans and went quickly to tell Paul. His enemies were planning to trap him that very night, so Paul had to work with speed with what he had on hand.

He found a basket in the pantry, a very large wash basket which could have held laundry for a family of 10. He, being small, could just fit into it, so he tucked himself in while the disciples covered him with a red-checked tablecloth.

You might think this basket looked a bit suspicious. You're right. After all, it would have to be a pretty big basket to hold an apostle. But God was with them. Only once did a soldier stop them and ask what was in the basket. The two disciples who were carrying the basket by its handles had a moment of heart flurries.

"Oh, just 42 loaves of Italian bread, 7 strings of salami, and a whole lot of dill pickles for a wedding party," said one disciple, casually. The other whistled and looked up into the air.

The soldier nodded and waved them on. Once they reached the city wall, they hoisted the basket up and lowered it down over the other side by rope. The rope snapped just before Paul landed.

Paul went to Jerusalem and he wasn't welcome there either. So he went back to his hometown of Tarsus and took up his trade of tentmaking. He thought he would wait there until the Lord told him where to go.

Before long Barnabas, a Christian friend, came to him and persuaded him to go with him to Antioch in Syria, where they could preach about Christ to those who didn't know him at all. It was a new challenge, and Paul soaked up challenges like a blotter does ink, so off they went.

They worked for a year in Antioch and, for the first time, Paul had great success. They left a community of Christians behind, the first of many more to come. And Antioch was his jumping-off place. For 20-some more years, he traveled hundreds—thousands—of miles, touching every bustling city, marketplace, or tiny rest-stop watering hole. He convinced an uncountable number of souls to be warmed in God's love and to let it soak in and cover every part of their lives.

He journeyed to Corinth and Ephesus and Thessalonica, and from there to Galatia and Malta and Cyprus. And after he founded churches in all those places, he thought he'd see what he could do in Crete and Athens and Syracuse. Someone once wrote that he planted churches the way Johnny Appleseed planted trees.

When he wasn't on the road, he was writing letters to the brothers and sisters he had left behind in those communities. His letters were those of a loving father, who cared enough about his children to scold them and urge them to do better. He patted them on the back and then tweaked their noses.

He never asked more of them than he did of himself. He was their leader (although sometimes nagging, impatient leader) who could not bear to see anyone poke along the road. He wanted them to stride with great vigor, "pressing on to the goal, to the prize of God's heavenly calling!" There were to be no stops for snoozes or buying popcorn.

Paul's spirit kept his body going. He was sick on and off all his life. He didn't eat what was good for him, and he couldn't bear to waste time sleeping, and his nose was always either nipped by frost or burned by the sun. His nerves never had a moment's rest, for he was always just one jump ahead of the local sheriff who wanted to chase him out of town for disturbing the peace.

Yet, by God's grace, Paul persevered. On five different occasions the Jews gave him thirty-nine lashes across his back. He was beaten by rods, was stoned and even shipwrecked three times. Many times and in many ways he was in danger and distress during his tireless travels.

Paul loved to tell these stories of his adventures. If sometimes his tales of how he escaped shipwrecks and snakes and jails sound somewhat puffed-up, I don't think he meant to be boastful about himself. Rather, he wanted to show that the glory of his wiggling out of these incredible escapades belongs to God. The only way he could come out on top of them was because Christ was with him and in him.

"It is no longer I who live but Christ who lives in me!" he would explain.

The time came, however, when there would be no last-minute escape. The Emperor Nero decided to silence Paul for good and ordered him beheaded. From his Roman jail Paul wrote his friend Timothy, "I am even now ready to be offered; the time of my departure is at hand. But," and you can almost see his eyes light up, "I have fought a good fight; I have finished my course; I have kept the faith!"

And so, on a road outside the gates of Rome, Paul lost his head. I'm sure, if he had had the pen and paper and time, he would have recorded that it was of much more importance that he lost his heart to Christ on that road to Damascus many years ago.

If you'd like to curl up some rainy afternoon and read Paul's letters for yourself, you will find them at the end of the New Testament in the Bible. Don't worry if you don't understand them all or trip over the names of cities. You will find some small part which you feel Paul was writing for *you*, as well as those long-ago Christians.

He will remind you that "whatever you do, work at it with your whole being and do it for the Lord!"

For the Lord and not for the reward, which is nice but not necessary. So when you shovel snow, scour the bathtub because the bather before you didn't, study French, empty the kitty litter, make Jello, mind your whiny sister or write a thank-you to Aunt Kathy who always sends you underwear for your birthday—don't expect money or praise or a favor in return. Do it with your whole being for the Lord.

Like Paul, *press on* to the heavenly goal!

Thomas the Apostle

July 3

There was once a saint called Doubting Thomas who was very bothersome to live with because he was a skeptic. He was one of our Lord's 12 apostles, so you'd think he would know better than to be a skeptic. A skeptic, in case you might not know, is someone who doesn't believe anything you tell him unless he sees it for himself.

"Show me! Prove it!" Thomas would say with a cool eye and a bored look. "If I can't see it, touch it, smell it, I don't believe it."

If Peter would say, "Tomorrow should be a good day for fishing because the sunset today was a beautiful red—" (you know, ". . . red at night, sailor's delight"), Thomas would answer, "I don't know about that. It could just as easily rain."

Or, if Philip would bring in a nice warm egg, fresh from the hen, for breakfast, Thomas would look at it, feel it and shrug, "How do you know it is fresh? She could have been sitting on it for three days and that's why it's warm."

So you can see, Thomas could be a trial to the other apostles. But they loved him even during his worst questioning. They knew they also had faults which probably bothered him.

Thomas even questioned our Lord's rising from the tomb on the first Easter morning. The evening of that happy day, Jesus appeared to the apostles in their locked room (they were frightened because they hadn't met the Holy Spirit yet), but Thomas was off on an errand.

They couldn't wait to tell Thomas. He listened to them with his cool manner and then sniffed, "I think you've been seeing things. There is no way I'll believe he was here. We've all been under a strain, you know—I think it's all wishful thinking."

A week later, Jesus appeared to them again, walking right through the door and up to Thomas. "I bring you my peace, Thomas," he said to his startled apostle. He showed his hands to him.

"Look, Thomas, do you see the scars from the nails? And give me your hand; put it in my side. Do you feel the wound and see the blood? Do you believe now, Doubting Thomas?"

Thomas could not look at our Lord. He hung his head and was very, very ashamed that he had so little faith. If he could believe that apple blossoms could turn into apples why could he not believe that Jesus could be standing here alive and well, sharing their meal?

He fell to Jesus' feet and covered his eyes. "My Lord and my God," he whispered, "I believe!"

Jesus smiled and said, "Now that you've seen me, Thomas, you believe. But how much more blessed are they who have not seen and yet believe. Think about that."

So Thomas thought about it and made up his mind from that moment on, he would not be a skeptic.

He no longer said "Show me!" or "Prove it!" If someone told him that eggplants in Mongolia grew in the shape of bananas, he would nod his head and reply, "That is very interesting, and I really would like to see one." This made life easier for everyone, including Thomas.

Now he had to use all his energy and wit for preaching to strangers

instead of arguing with friends. After Pentecost, the apostles spread out to bring Christ's word to the rest of the world. Legend says that our Lord appeared to Thomas again and told him that he would like him to go to India, which was not one of Thomas's favorite places.

"Oh, Lord," he groaned, "send me anywhere else. Thuringia— Lapland—Northumbria—Westphalia—but not *India*!"

Jesus said, "India, Thomas. Don't worry, I will watch over you while you go tell everyone we are all brothers and sisters with one Father."

And Thomas remembered about believing without seeing, so he packed his bag for India.

After he got used to it, Thomas came to love his new home and the kind, loving people who lived in it and who soaked up God's word like sunshine. He could see how, as always, God's will was wiser than his own desire.

Thomas made such a name for himself he even impressed the king, whose name was Gundafor. One day Gundafor called Thomas to his palace and asked him what else he could do besides talk about this God the king didn't know.

"Well," said Thomas, "I can build houses and make plows and oars and shipmasts and carve tombs and . . ."

"That's enough," said the king. "I've been looking for the right person to build me a new palace. The one we have now is getting cramped and the children need more room. You'll have to make the swimming pool larger, and I'd like a few extra rooms for a bakery and a cheese house, a library with a stained-glass door, a rabbit hutch and a tree-house, of course. Well, here are the plans and some money for you to buy what you need."

Gundafor left Thomas with a huge bag of gold and told him he would be back in a few months after a trip to Persia. Thomas looked at all that money and thought of what Jesus said about laying up treasure in heaven instead of on earth. He decided to do a marvelous thing for the king. He gave all the money away to the poor, every bit of it.

When Gundafor returned, he went right to Thomas, saying, "I can't wait to see my new palace. I've been thinking of nothing else all the way home."

"Well, your Highness," said Thomas, taking a deep breath, "your palace is waiting for you but you can't see it now. Only when you have left this world."

"What! I can't see it *now*? Where is it?" asked the king, sounding annoyed.

"It's in heaven. I have laid up a treasure for you that will never rot or be destroyed by wind or rain or moths. I gave your money to your poor subjects in Christ's name. And now your mansion in heaven is beyond anything I could ever build. Stained-glass windows as well as doors . . ."

The king wanted his palace *now*. "Show me! Prove it!" he roared. Since Thomas couldn't do either, Gundafor cast him into prison. "Tomorrow you shall die for stealing my money. This is nothing but a Christian trick."

That night Gundafor's brother, who had recently died and gone to heaven, came back to earth to tell Gundafor about the beautiful palace awaiting him, with a bower of honeysuckle climbing up the stained-glass door and a goldfish pond in the back yard. "You can't believe how nice it is, my brother. Would you mind if I used it now since you don't need it yet?" And the brother vanished without waiting for an answer.

Gundafor was stunned and could say nothing. Then he realized what Thomas had been trying to tell him. Gundafor freed Thomas at once and asked him to baptize the entire royal family that very day.

He told Thomas how sorry he was for having doubted him, and Thomas just smiled and said not to worry about it. After all, who could understand better than one who once was known as Doubting Thomas?

*O*ur *L*ady of *K*nock

August 21

Usually, Mary has a specific reason for stopping by and shaking up our lives. She may come to comfort or guide or admonish or rescue or deliver a message from her Son. Sometimes she just asks that a church be built in her honor. But there is always a reason.

Yet, when she appeared at a church in the village of Knock in Ireland, she said nothing, did nothing, asked nothing. Why then did she come to this remote rural place of "forgotten fields and rural farmhouses"? It was no different from any such suffering village of that time, certainly not a place you'd expect a queen to visit. But then, Mary doesn't go by *our* standards of beauty or acceptability.

Ireland in the mid-nineteenth century was a sorry land of sickness, famine and despair. When we think of famine today, we see the skin-and-bones children of Africa, not farm families in the lush green fields of Ireland. But in 1846 a blight caused the failure of the country's main crop, potatoes, and many people died of starvation because of it.

Others died from the diseases of typhus and cholera. Greedy landlords evicted the tenants who could not pay their rent, and broken families lived in workhouse shelters or emigrated to England or America. Ireland had little comfort or hope throughout the nineteenth century.

On the night of August 21, 1879, our Lady came and delivered both comfort and hope when she appeared for a few hours at the village church of Saint John the Baptist. It was a small place that held thirty people at best, and two statues, one of Mary and the other of Joseph.

The pastor, Father Cavanaugh, was a well-loved and good man who was as poor as his congregation. He sold all he had of value—his watch, his horse—to help them. When he died, it was written in his obituary that he never had a bank account because he had nothing to put into it. And he had a deep love for the Immaculate Conception. Many people believe Mary came to Knock because of the pastor's affection for her.

A year before our Lady appeared here, a storm had done much damage to the little church, smashing windows and the two statues. Father Cavanaugh ordered new ones, which were finally put into place on that hot, muggy day of August 21.

It was a day of routine work. Some villagers were haying, mothers were hanging laundry, others were cutting turf squares from the peat bog for winter fuel. By midday, the sun disappeared and rains began, first in a drizzle, then in a downpour. By suppertime, Father Cavanaugh arrived home after visiting parishioners, soaked to the bone. His housekeeper, Mary McLoughlin, lit a fire, and he huddled by it trying to dry out his wet clothes and shivering body.

About 8:30 p.m., her work done, Mary left the rectory to visit her friend, Margaret Beirne. A good hot cup of tea and friendly exchange of news was just what she needed on such a miserable night. As she passed by the northern gable of the church, she noticed several statues sitting in the churchyard bathed in an unusual light—in the rain. She wondered why the pastor had ordered new statues when he already had replaced the broken ones. She thought it all very strange but put it out of her mind.

After an hour of tea and chatter with her friend, Mary returned to the rectory, accompanied by Margaret's daughter, Mary, who wanted to be sure she got home safely. When they reached the churchyard, the bright light was still shining over the statues. As they moved closer to inspect the scene, the statues began to move, and Mary McLoughlin gasped, "Dear God, they're not statues! Look, there is the Blessed Virgin!"

The two Marys, quite befuddled, their minds unable to accept what their eyes saw, knelt down in the wet grass, speechless. What did they see? Three figures dressed in silvery white robes, suspended two feet above the ground at the gable wall. Mary was in the center, her robe covered with a white cloak that fastened at the throat. She wore a crown of glittering gold crosses, and in the center of the crown, on her forehead, was a rose. Her expression was pleasant, her hands held up and outward. Her feet were bare.

To her right was Saint Joseph with gray beard and hair, his head inclined toward her. To her left was Saint John the Evangelist, dressed as a bishop, with a book in his left hand and his right hand raised, as if preaching. To the left of Saint John was an altar on which a lamb faced the figures, and behind the lamb was a cross.

The two women stood up and said nothing until the housekeeper told the young girl to run home and get her family, tell neighbors, bring people back to make sure they were really seeing what they thought they saw.

Mary Beirne did just that. Her brother, Dominick, first laughed and shook his head over such nonsense. Then he tried to stop her, "before she makes a fool of herself in front of everyone!" But there was no stopping Mary, who banged on doors and made sure anyone who could move would follow her to see the incredible sight.

Soon a small crowd of twenty-two people had gathered in the churchyard. Their ages ranged from five to seventy-five years. These were simple, no-nonsense, hardworking people, not inclined toward visions or fancies. But they too stared awestruck and confirmed what the two Marys had seen.

"The figures were full and round as if they had a body and life," said one. One boy saw "angels hovering during the whole time . . . I saw their wings fluttering." An old lady tried to kiss our Lady's bare feet, but she found she had nothing in her hands but the wall.

One little boy saw a halo of angels circling the head of the lamb, and another wanted to take "the shining people" home with him.

The vision was still there when Mary McLoughlin hurried to the rectory to tell Father Cavanaugh and beg him to come see for himself. But he did not. He was weary and wet and, to tell the truth, he did not believe Mary. He thought the vision might be because of her "little fault." As one writer put it, "Mary . . . occasionally drank a little more whiskey than was fitting for . . . a housekeeper." But later, when he learned of the appearance from other viewers, he was heartsore that he had not gone to see for himself.

The news spread like wildfire, as such stories do in small villages. Ten days after the vision, cases of paralysis, cancer, blindness, tuberculosis were cured by drinking the water with bits of mortar from the gable in it. Pilgrims began coming from all over Ireland, some walking the distance barefoot.

Most of the clergy did not approve of the goings on at Knock, but Father Cavanaugh believed firmly in the truth of our Lady's visit, even if he had not seen her himself. He knew his flock; he was their *anam-chara*, "soul-friend," and he would know if they were not telling the truth.

Through the years, the people who saw the vision were interviewed by theologians and scholars, and by 1936, those who were still living were quite old, but not one of them changed or denied what they had seen. Said one, "I will remember what I saw that night till I die."

There were so many cures reported that Father Cavanaugh had to keep a diary of them. He told the pilgrims that Knock was destined to bring people from every part of the world. That seemed a wishful fantasy then, but today, over a century later, they still come, over a million a year. On the one hundredth anniversary of the appearance, Pope John Paul II came and blessed the shrine at Knock, known in Gaelic as *Cnoc Mhuire*, Mary's Holy Hill.

The answer to why she came is still a mystery. Some say it was to give hope to the weary, faithful people, to let them know Ireland was in her loving care. Some say the message of Knock is a biblical one, that the description of Mary's appearance as a "woman clothed with the sun, with the moon under her feet and on her head is a crown of twelve stars" is from John's writing in the Book of Revelation.

But for many others, our Lady's visit is like the comfort of the good friend who comes unsummoned in times of need or distress, who embraces us warmly and listens to us with understanding love. Such a love has no need of speech.

Cosmas and Damian

September 26

Once upon a time, there were twin brothers who did everything together from the moment they were born. They took their first steps, running to their mother, at the same time. They woke at 6 a.m. together, rubbed their eyes and scratched their heads together, and always wanted Cream of Wheat for breakfast on the same days. They even made holes in the toes of their socks at the same time. So when one brother said, "I think I'm going to be a saint," the other, of course, replied, "Why, I was just thinking the same thing!"

Their names were Cosmas and Damian and they were born into a wealthy family of Arabia nearly 300 years after Christ died. When they were toddlers, bouncing about like two peas in a pod, their father died. They missed him terribly. Even though they were Christians and tried to be brave, the boys would go to their rooms and cry in the dark because they didn't have a father.

Their mother told them to dry their eyes because they *did* have a father who was the King of Heaven. Since he was a king, they were royal children and must always act as a king's sons. They must fill their lives with noble deeds and help the weak and the sick and the lonely.

The boys grew up, enjoying their secret and trying to live up to it. They were sons of a king! They decided to become doctors—together, of course—doctors for the poor as well as the rich. Not only were there uncountable poor people in their land, but also a great deal of sickness of all variety. And there were not enough doctors. Only the very wealthy could afford to have a doctor living in their palaces, and they certainly didn't want poor people coming there, scuffing up the floors and putting dirty fingermarks on the walls.

So Cosmas and Damian studied for years with the most learned men of medicine. They were taught how to set broken limbs and lower fevers and massage away aches. They discovered the herbs and grasses and flowers that would help heal and cure, and they learned how sick and unhappy minds often made the body act the same way.

They cared for rich and poor alike, and even for animals. After all, as Damian said, "People can speak and complain of their sickness. But those dumb creatures, also made by our King, can only suffer in silence."

The brothers taught people not to fuss over themselves or take to their beds at the first sign of sniffles but to be sensible and use God's natural gifts. They carried wild horseradish roots and cloves of garlic for people with clogged up heads. "There you are," they'd tell them as they wheezed and sneezed, "*this* will clean out your sinuses!"

So their days were busy from sunrise to sunset. They mixed yarrow with cobwebs to stop bleeding wounds, and put castor oil on warts and corns and bathed sore eyes with eyebright tea. Wherever they were, people found them and came in a steady stream: ladies with headaches and carpenters with smashed thumbs, girls with hiccups and boys with black eyes, a bear with a bee-stung nose, a camel with cramp. No one, person or beast, was ever turned away.

The brothers asked only one thing of their patients: They could make no payment for their healing. Cosmas and Damian told them it was the work which God had given them to do, and as God asked no payment for the gifts he gave, neither would they.

Sometimes it is harder to receive a gift than to give one, especially when you are so grateful you want to do *something* to say thank you. One day a woman whom the brothers had cured of a dizziness, which made her tilt to one side and feel as though the sky was falling in on her, could not contain her happiness.

She offered them a sack with three fresh eggs in it, begging them to please accept it.

Cosmas walked away, and the woman turned to Damian. "Please, sir, you have cured my dizzy tilt and I can see the world as it is again. Won't you please take these eggs and enjoy them? I ask you in Jesus' name!"

When Damian heard that, his heart was touched. How could he refuse her without being rude to our Lord? So he took the eggs and brought them home. When Cosmas saw them, he became very angry. For the first time in their lives, the brothers did not agree.

"Damian," Cosmas asked, "how could you do this? You know we made a vow never to take payment for any good we do. How could you take these eggs from that poor woman?"

He turned from his brother, refusing to share the room with him, and went outdoors to sleep.

That night, God crept into Cosmas' dreams, into his very heart, and asked, "Cosmas, my son, why are you so angry at your brother?"

"Lord," he answered, "You know why. He went back on his word. You know our vow!"

"Cosmas, you are thinking just with your head. Do not be so stiff-necked and proud that you must follow the letter of your own law. Was it not in my name that Damian took the eggs? The woman gave them in love for me and in thanks to you for letting me work through you. Don't you see? Your brother is wiser than you."

Cosmas woke and thought with his heart. He went quickly to his brother and gave him a bear hug, which woke Damian up very quickly. Damian forgave him, for he understood.

(Sometimes we decide to do something for Christ and won't budge an inch because that's the way *we* want it, even if we make other people unhappy. We may decide to offer up chocolate chip cookies because we *love* chocolate chip cookies. And then we visit a lonely old lady who loves to bake cookies for company. Her eyes light up with pleasure when she offers us one and we must decide quickly. Do we say, "No, thank you," so we can say with pride, "I never slipped *once*"? Or do we think of her feelings and eat the cookies, telling her how absolutely delicious they are? We must decide, as Damian did, to act as our Lord would in the same situation.)

The brothers' fame began to spread throughout Arabia, and this angered the ruler, who was not a Christian. These brothers would turn the whole country Christian if they went about healing and comforting and doing good. They must be stopped, he decided.

He ordered Cosmas and Damian to be seized and cast into the sea. They were hustled off to a cliff overlooking the cold gray water.

Here the soldiers bound their hands and feet and threw them into the wild, churning waves.

Immediately, so they say, the sea turned quiet and blue and the wind became gentle as a sigh. The brothers rose to the surface of the water, their hands and feet freed, and walked toward the shore, each led by an angel who surrounded them with a protecting light.

The ruler was very angry at this, and a bit frightened. He certainly didn't want the Christians to prove that there was a God who cared enough about them to send his angels to guard them. He ordered that they be cast into a roaring fire and thought that would be the last of them.

As soon as Cosmas and Damian were thrown into the flaming mass, the fire flickered and grew dim, until only a faint gray ash was left. The brothers stepped out—not burnt to a crisp, but just nicely pink and healthy-looking.

Then the ruler, very, very angry by now, ordered them to be bound to crosses and stoned to death by the soldiers. But as the stones flew through the air, they turned back and bounced off the soldiers who had thrown them. Before long, the ground was littered with men groaning and holding their heads. Cosmas whispered to Damian, "Somebody should send for a doctor!"

Once again, the ruler tried. He ordered archers to shoot their arrows into the hearts of the brothers, but the arrows also changed direction and returned to chase the archers. They dropped their bows and fell to the ground, hoping the arrows would zoom by and miss them.

Finally, the ruler declared that these men were magicians. Since magic was made by the mind, he would simply relieve them of their minds. He ordered Cosmas and Damian to be beheaded, and so they were.

Cosmas and Damian lost their heads for God. They had given him their hearts long ago; and now, bodies and souls, they came back altogether to him. And they didn't stop their healing just because they were in heaven. They were incurable curers. People who prayed to them were healed, or the brothers would appear to the sick in their dreams and tell them where to find valerian root for their nerves and wild ginger for their upset stomachs.

Cosmas and Damian have left us more than the stories of their healing. They have taught us how to act as children of the King. They have shown us that we are to think first of serving God and his people, to use our talents and not be concerned what we get in the way of money or honor.

When we do something we know is absolutely wonderful, we don't stand around with our hands in our pockets, waiting to be told how absolutely wonderful we are. Royal children don't need rewards. We've already inherited heaven!

Vincent de Paul

September 27

Once upon a time, there was a boy named Vincent who tried to fool God. He thought he could pretend to be someone he wasn't, and no one would ever know. Because he was a poor boy who hated being poor, he told himself that he would become a priest. Then he would have a comfortable life, with plenty of food and his own home, and everyone would look up to him. He would be the master instead of the servant.

But Vincent forgot that God has a sense of humor that can turn the tables on the best of plans. He listened to the thoughts in Vincent's mind and chuckled. "Very well, my son, you shall be a priest. More than that, you will be a saint, my saint of the poor!"

Vincent, who had been born in a peasant family in France, wanted so much to escape his life of poverty that he lay awake nights on his straw cot, planning ways to change it. He did not like tending sheep and pigs all day at the mercy of the wind and sun and rain. He wanted to be comfortable, to wear clean, warm clothes and eat roast chicken and drink good red wine—just like the village priest!

There was no reason he couldn't be a priest. He was smart and he wasn't wicked even if he wasn't very holy either. And in return for this good life, he would do everything he was supposed to do: He would say Mass and baptize babies and bless the vineyards and visit the old ladies of the parish, who would give him French bread and sausage to take home. It would be a good life for everybody.

So Vincent worked hard and before he knew it, he was 24 years old and had been ordained a priest. His dream had come true. Then one fine spring day, he went on a business trip to Marseilles, a seaport town. He finished his work early and decided to come home by boat, since he had the time to enjoy it. The wind was calm and the sun bright. What a pleasant afternoon he would have!

But within the hour, his happiness turned to fear. His heart nearly stopped in fright. The boat was seized and captured by Turkish pirates, who took over the wheel and steered it in the opposite direction to Tunisia, where the passengers would be sold as slaves.

God had begun to play his joke in a rather rough fashion. Vincent, who had been heading for a life of comfort, was led by a chain about his neck to the center of town where merchants could buy the captive they wanted. He was bought first by a fisherman, who then sold him to a doctor, who sold him to a farmer. He and the farmer became friends (Vincent discovered he had once been a Christian), and they decided to try to slip out of the country together. They waited and planned for 10 months before they had the chance to steal a boat and escape in the night to France.

In the two years he had been a slave, God's grace had sparked the beginning of a change in Vincent's heart. The hardships, the struggles, the sufferings of the slaves had stirred something in his soul. He understood them. He had been poor; how could he ever turn his back on that life and not try to change it? He had been able to help the suffering poor in a foreign land. Should he not do the same for his own peasant countrymen in France?

So he came to Paris when he was 27 and met a holy priest named Father Pierre de Berulle, who would guide him to his life's work. Father Pierre saw something special in this young man and felt that God had a definite mission for him, even if he didn't know what it was. When he heard that a wealthy family was in need of a priest for their household, he was sure this was a job for Vincent. So off went the young priest to the household of the de Gondi family.

The de Gondis owned magnificent homes in town and in the country, with huge estates of woods and gardens and trout streams. Vincent was their chaplain and the tutor for the children and he helped in the physical and spiritual care of the servants and workers who took care of the family.

There were so many workers, Vincent banded them together into one big parish. Madame de Gondi approved of this. It relieved her conscience to know that the peasants for whom the family was responsible were being cared for. Soon the work became almost too much for one man. Vincent realized this was work for a special group of priests, a different kind of order (or "company" as he called them), who would devote themselves to the care of poor country people. They should live in a community but not be separated from the world.

He spoke of this to Madame de Gondi, who immediately gathered up a bundle of money and told him to go ahead and *do it*. So he did. He organized a band of priests who would live and work among the poor and called them the Congregation of the Missions (or Vincentians, as we know them now). He, and they, then helped the people of the parish remember that they were brothers and sisters with one Father. They sought out the needy and helped them. Everyone. "Remember," Vincent told them, "that our Lord said, 'Whatsoever you do to these, the least of my brethren, you do to me.' "

The new company found an old estate in Paris which was called St. Lazare because it had once been used to take care of lepers. For 28 years, this was Vincent's headquarters and home. Here he directed his "sons" (and later his "daughters," the Sisters of Charity), wrote his letters, held retreats, and thought up plans to make a better life for the poor.

Before the Sisters of Charity came the Ladies of Charity. These were a group of wealthy, aristocratic women of Paris who were brought together by Vincent's friend Louise de Marillac. Louise had been shaken by the fire of this zealous young priest, who called for the rich to consider their cold and hungry brothers and sisters. She and the ladies were gracious and gave parties and teas to raise money for the poor, and that helped.

But the Ladies were not nurses and had families of their own to tend to. So Louise gathered together and taught young women from the country, who became nurses and teachers and household workers. They were the first band of sisters dedicated to taking care of God's poor. The Sisters of Charity, like the Vincentians, were to live in a community but work in the city with the sick and needy. Vincent wanted no collection of nuns who shut themselves away from the world.

"Your convent will be the house of the sick," he said; "your cell, a hired room; your cloister, the streets of the city or the wards of the hospital."

Soon the Sisters were working everywhere, in hospitals, orphanages, prisons, even in armies. Vincent's "companies" soon became known outside France and spread throughout Europe, Africa and, eventually, America. Then, 200 years after Vincent died, Frederic Ozanam formed the Society of St. Vincent de Paul, a gathering of Catholic laity which continues the practice of loving charity as given to them by "Monsieur Vincent," as he came to be called by the people of Paris.

They loved him as much as he loved them and the city itself. He came to know Paris first as a young priest on horseback, discovering every abandoned child, every beggar or convict who needed help. Then, when he could no longer ride, he walked and poked about with a cane. He loved every inch of his city. He became the priest of a small church to which fishermen, farmers and laborers came. The little church is still standing, and in its garden is a very old tree said to have been planted by Monsieur Vincent himself.

He sometimes tried the patience of those who worked with him, for he was not a naturally good-humored man. He was impatient and quick-tempered and, "but for divine grace," he admitted, "I would have been in temper hard and repellent, rough and crabbed." He was short and squat, with a broad jaw and short beard. His dark brown eyes shone from under black brows that were heavy as an awning. And his nose was very large and like a bulb.

Sometimes he was slow in making a decision. He always wanted

to be sure that what he wanted to do was the will of God. He would not be pushed. "Do not tread on the heels of Providence, who is our guide," he would say. But once he made up his mind that something was God's will, he couldn't be stopped from putting his thoughts into action.

Vincent's idea of charity was that people should take care of each other, person to person, as they saw the need. He didn't believe in leaving it to a government or charity far away. He did believe that the parish and the priest should be the center of our lives, not just on Sunday but every moment; that way we would remember that we are all members of a single family and children of the same heavenly Father.

He gave whatever he had to anyone, without worrying whether it was going to the "right" people. They were all the "right" people. Slaves, orphans, the rejected and despised—all were in his care. "In a poor man," he said, "I do not notice his rough outside, his coarseness . . . , but I look at the reverse . . . . I see nothing save the Son of God, poor by his own choice."

Vincent showed us *how* to give. It is not enough to give money for a poor baby in Bolivia. Good, but not *enough*. We must also think of our neighbor who may have nothing left on his shelves but half a box of soggy cornflakes and a can of spinach and is too proud to let anyone know his stomach is hurting. As you sit here, munching a cracker with peanut butter, it is hard to imagine anyone being that hungry. But *try*. Try to imagine for Sunday dinner a can of spinach that looks like wet, dead seaweed. And that is it. And for Monday's dinner, limp cornflakes.

147

Vincent sought out the old and lonely (and the young and lonely) and gave them eggs and milk and cabbage and cheese to go with the spinach. He gave himself, his company, his caring. If someone needed a coat, he took off his and gave it. (And he didn't stop to cut off the buttons or the lining in case he might use them sometime.) And when rich people gave him old shoes, he would ask them to make sure they came in pairs. "You know," he would smile, "you'd be surprised to see how few people there are with one foot!" He asked them to give with their whole hearts, and not just to give things they wouldn't use themselves, for what was the sacrifice in that?

Vincent was very much an ordinary man. He saw no visions, performed no miracles, changed nothing but himself. The boy who vowed he would never be poor became the man who chose his home in the midst of the poor.

By the time he reached heaven, he had lost all desire to become the comfortable master of the manor. He had found his place instead as God's handyman, the holy caretaker who patched up frostbitten lives.

Monsieur Vincent, keep us from ever being too comfortable, and give us the grace to be caretakers, too!

The Heavenly Helpers

September 29

They say our Lord
On his throne in heaven
Is circled by angels
In a ring of seven.

Of this holy band
Three we know well:
Michael and Gabriel
And, of course, Raphael.

What did they do,
These angelic three,
Who touched the earth
Infrequently?

Michael the Avenger banished Satan,
Who preened himself as Prince,
Flung him from heaven to the pit of hell,
And he's been there ever since.
Michael the Protector
Saved Isaac from the knife,
Scattered death on Egypt
To give the Jews life.

Michael the Guardian
Warned Joseph to flee in the dark
To foil cruel Herod
Before the song of the lark.

Gabriel brought tidings
Of the first Christmas morn,
With a vision to Zachary
Of John-to-be-born.
He called on Mary,
As she knelt in the sod,
And gently addressed her
As *Mother of God!*
And when Jesus was born
Gabriel's trumpet shattered the night
And he cheered the shepherds
Cowed in fright.
"Rejoice, fear not,"
His song sang out bold,
"Your Savior is here—
Come out of the cold!"

And Raphael the Healer
To blind Tobias gave sight,
Then walked as guardian
With his son, day and night.
Raphael saved the son
From a monstrous fish,

Then led him to Sarah,
The bride he had wished.
And when Our Lord wept
In Gethsemani's wood,
Raphael consoled him
And blotted the blood.

So if you tangle with Satan
And must do battle,
Call on Michael
So your teeth won't rattle.

And if you bring tidings
By song or by quote,
Gabriel will clear out
The frogs in your throat.

And if you must go
On a trip of import,
Go with Raphael,
Heavenly escort.

Don't forget
These angelic three!
They wait for your call
Or sob or plea,
As they sit on their pins
In eternity.

*T*herese

October 1

Once upon a time, there was a little girl who was determined to have her own way. When she wanted something, she wanted all of it, no bits or pieces or sips or samples. She wanted *the whole thing*, whether it was a cookie or a box of ribbons or her parents' attention. And because she was the baby of the family, she usually got it.

So when Therese (that was her name) decided that the one thing she wanted in this life was to be a saint, nothing could stop her. She didn't say, "Well, maybe tomorrow, or the day after when I start to feel holy, I'll start," or "When I enter the convent and have time to pray a lot, I'll think about it." She used everything, the whole of her life, for holiness from that moment on.

Therese was like every baby sister you've ever known. She was fussed over and coddled and shown off, with good reason. She was quite pretty, with a mass of golden curls and blue-gray eyes. She had such a way of commanding attention, her father called her his Little Queen. But she was such a charming child people smiled even as they did exactly as she wished.

Her full name was Marie Frances Therese and she was the youngest child of Louis and Zelie Martin. Her father was a well-to-do clockmaker and her mother made the beautiful lace for which their town of Alencon was noted. Her parents loved each other deeply,

almost as much as they loved God. When they married, their first prayer was for many children who would become saints.

They gathered a nice large houseful, nine in all. Four children died when they were babies, but their parents did not grieve. They were graced with a faith that helped them rejoice that their little ones had already gained heaven and would be waiting to greet them when they arrived. And, after all, they did have five daughters here on earth to raise.

The eldest was Marie, followed by Pauline, and then Leonie and Celine and, finally, Therese. The baby of the family never wanted for someone to push her on the swing, tie her shoelaces or get her a drink during the night. Sometimes it seemed as if she had five mothers taking care of her.

The sister she loved most dearly was Celine. They did everything together. They giggled and had secrets and made hand shadows on the walls and teased each other. Often Therese would climb out of her bed at night and jump in with Celine. In the morning she would hug her tightly and beg the maid, Louise, to let her stay with her big sister. "Can't you see we are like two little white chickens and we must always be together?"

Once, when Therese was small, Leonie brought a basket of out-grown toys and said she and Celine might choose one apiece, since they had been good that morning. Celine took forever to pick, and just when Therese was about to burst with impatience, she chose a fuzzy white rabbit. Therese quickly snatched the basket out of her hands and held it tightly to her chest. "I choose *everything*!" she snapped, and marched out of the room with her prize.

Of course she brought it back in a matter of moments, for even though she was sometimes selfish, she was just as quick to be sorry and smother someone she had hurt with kisses.

The Martins were a happy family, full of love and delight in having each other around. But when Therese was four, her mother died and their lives were changed forever. Pauline became her Little Mother (and Marie was Celine's). Their father grieved for his wife, even though he knew that she was happy in heaven. He did not want to stay in their home, so full of family memories, so he sold his business and moved his family to the town of Lisieux.

He found a lovely old house called *Les Buissonets* (The Elms) which perked up everyone's spirits. It was a perfect home for romping and growing up in, with secret nooks and window seats to curl up on and read or dream or pray. Marie ran the house and Pauline took charge of teaching the others their lessons and prayers. She would read aloud to them at night, stories from the Gospels or the lives of the saints, and Therese's soul soaked it up as a thirsty rose would water.

When Therese was nine, Pauline left The Elms to enter the convent of the Carmelites at Lisieux. Therese thought her heart would break to lose her Little Mother. Then, with her whole-hearted determination, she decided that this would be her life and that she would enter the convent also. She had known in her heart for some time that God wanted her to give her life completely to him. She wanted with all her being to offer her life for poor souls who were hurt or lonely or angry or full of hate, and who had no one to pray for them. But she had a while to wait.

When she was 14, her sister Marie joined Pauline in the convent, and soon after Leonie left to become a Visitation nun. That left only Celine and Therese home to take care of their father. The desire to become a Carmelite had grown stronger until Therese could not bear to keep it to herself any longer. She had to go as soon as possible!

But what of her father? How could she leave him while he was still so sad from her mother's death? Gently, almost fearfully, she told him how she felt. Her father drew her to him, and with tears in his eyes (and his heart no doubt aching), Louis Martin told his daughter of the great joy she had given him with her news. It could not have been easy for him to lose his Little Queen, but he remembered that he and Zelie had prayed for children who would someday be saints. How could he hold this eager one back?

But even though he was willing and gave Therese his blessing, the nuns at the convent, her parish priest and the Bishop were not so agreeable. They said she could not enter the convent until she was *at least* 18 years old. Since their word was final, the only one who could change their minds was the Pope himself.

Very well, then, they would make the pilgrimage to Rome. Therese and Celine and their father arrived in Rome with the request for an audience. It was granted and Therese, who was not yet 15, became frightened at what she was about to do. She was awed at the thought of speaking with the Pope and knew she would stammer and stutter and never get the words out right. But without his help she felt she would never get to join her sisters in the convent.

As she inched closer and closer in the line to see the Pope, she caught the eye of the priest from her parish who had refused her permission to enter the Carmelites. He must have read her mind, for he immediately announced in a loud voice that no one was to speak to the Holy Father.

Her heart beat loudly. She could hear it in her ears and feel it in her throat. She knew this was meant for her. She looked back at Celine. "Go ahead and speak!" urged her sister. Therese's turn had come and she went to her knees in front of the Pope.

"Most Holy Father," she pleaded, as fast as she could, "I want to ask you a great favor."

He bent down, his head almost touching hers, and his dark eyes met her wet ones.

"Please let me enter Carmel now even though I am only 15!" The priest behind the Pope was startled and angry. He interrupted Therese. "Your Holiness, this girl wishes to enter Carmel and her superiors are already going over the question."

"Very well, my child," said the Pope, "you must do what the superiors decide."

This wasn't enough for Therese. She wanted more, a definite *yes*. "*Please*, Holy Father! If you said yes, everyone else would be willing."

He gazed at her and said, feeling her hands clutching his knees, "Well, well, you will enter if it is God's will."

Her time was up, but Therese did not move. She prayed for the right words to move the Holy Father's heart. Two guards came over to lead her away, but she still would not move. She looked as stubborn as a dog who will not give up a bone. She clung tightly to the Pope's knees while the guards tried to tug her away. Finally the priest joined them, and the three men finally pulled her off and carried her out of the church.

Therese was hurt and puzzled. Surely Jesus had told her that he wanted her at Carmel. Thus, she reasoned simply, she must get there by any means. But she was beginning slowly to realize that she must let go of her strong will. She must let go and let God take care of it; she must trust him completely as a little child would her father.

She decided that she would offer herself to the Child Jesus as a plaything, a little ball to do with exactly as he liked. He could pick up this ball, throw it down, or let it roll far from him, but in the end, he would hold it close to his heart and never let it go again. Right now, she felt like a very sad little ball that had lost its bounce and was full of holes and abandoned.

But Jesus came quickly to rescue his plaything. The Bishop did give his permission, and when she was 15 years old, Therese joined Marie and Pauline in the convent at Lisieux. Here it was that Therese of the Child Jesus, the Little Flower as she called herself, bloomed with a sweet bright spirit for the nine years left of her life. She no longer had to fight the world to satisfy her will (which was now God's will). She had the *everything* she sought.

But she was still a fighter in the battle against herself. She set out to be a saint as deliberately as Joan of Arc set out to lead her army. She had always had an intense wish to be a Crusader or a missionary or, even better, a missionary martyr. She knew this was not to be. "Great deeds are not for me," she wrote. "I cannot preach the gospel or shed my blood. No matter. My brothers work in my stead, and I, a little child, stay close to the throne and love . . . . But how shall I show my love, since love proves itself by deeds? Well, the little child will strew flowers before Thee—that is, I will let no opportunity for sacrifice pass, no look, no work. I will make use of every little opportunity."

And she did. She did it so cheerfully, so quietly, hardly any of the sisters noticed her. When she was dying, the nuns shook their heads with pity and said what a shame it was that they couldn't find anything of importance to write about this little nun.

She did nothing unusual, nothing that would call attention to herself. She did the work given her, answered sharp remarks with kind ones, was friendly to those who were not. Her life was one of secret adventure, of giving to God a daily bouquet of offering up and giving in. No pinprick of annoyance was too small for Therese. She offered up being splashed by dirty laundry water with the same enthusiasm she offered up the cold.

She felt the cold deeply, right down into her bones. She would wrap herself in the thin blanket and shiver most of the night away in her damp room, but she would not ask for the comfort of another blanket. She would eat whatever was set before her, as is, whether the potatoes needed salt or the carrots were cooked to mush, and from the look on her face, you'd think it was apple pie and ice cream.

Therese likened her hidden life to that of the small white flower of springtime. She writes that when Jesus opened the book of nature to her, she saw that "every flower has a beauty of its own; that the splendor of the rose and the lily's whiteness do not deprive the violet of its scent . . . . So it is in the world of souls, the living garden of the Lord. It pleases him to create great saints, who may be compared with the lilies or the rose; but he has also created little ones, who must be content to be daisies or violets nestling at his feet . . . . Just as the sun shines equally on the cedar and the little flower, so the Divine Sun shines equally on everyone, great and small. . . .

"If a little flower could talk, it seems to me it would say what God has done for it quite simply and without concealment. It would not try to be humble by saying it was unattractive and without scent, that the sun had destroyed its freshness or the wind broken its stem, when all the time it knew it was quite the opposite."

Her sister, Pauline, who had become the Mother Superior of the convent, suspected that Therese was more than a simple, commonplace flower of a soul and ordered her to write the story of her life and of what Therese called her Little Way.

So, for the next 18 months, she sat on her stool every evening in her cold cell, writing and filling three large notebooks with this journal. She put down everything she felt would explain this Little Way and how we could all follow it.

"I want to seek a way to heaven, a new way, very short, very straight . . . , the way of trust and absolute self-surrender . . . .

"I am a very little soul, who can only offer very little things to Our Lord. I have not the courage to look through books for beautiful prayers. I do as a child who has not yet learned to read—I just tell our Lord all that I want and he understands."

While she was writing this journal, the nuns discovered that Therese was dying from tuberculosis, a disease which few survived at that time. Sometimes she was so weak she could barely dip her pen into her inkwell, so she was allowed to finish her journal in pencil. When it was done, she called it *The Story of a Soul*.

Therese's mission was to show us that God is our loving Father, not a stern taskmaster who sits with a frown, watching for us to make a mistake so he can pounce on us. He does not lie in wait to punish us because we ate the last Girl Scout cookie in the jug and lied about it. No matter what we do, Therese tells us, he is waiting and willing to forgive us.

Each of us has a mission from God, and as we grow older, he lets us know what it is. We may become tree surgeons or clam diggers or violin makers, according to our gifts. In everything we do, however, we may follow Therese's Little Way to heaven. All we need do is choose everything for our Lord! We may pick up a pin or wear socks that don't match or not stuff an apple core under the couch cushion. We may eat baked beans that have dried up and taste like bullets. Nothing is too small for the Little Way!

In September of her 24th year, Therese left this world but promised she would be back. "I have never given the good God anything but love, and it is with love he will repay. After my death, I will let fall a shower of roses. I will spend my heaven in doing good upon earth!"

So when you feel more like a dandelion gone to seed than a little white flower and you are certain someone has tied your shoelaces together as you try to find your way, don't give up! Pray to Therese and know that she will hear you.

Then open your heart and your hands to catch the petals!

Guardian Angels

Once upon a time, long before he made the world, God created pure spirits which he called angels. Their job was to praise him, to be his messengers and, the hardest job of all, to watch over all of us on earth once God made us.

They were smarter and more powerful than humans; they had to be if they were to be our guardians. God knew we would do lots of stumbling trying to get to heaven, so he gave each of us our own special angel to guide and protect us along our way. Can you imagine all the millions of people running to and fro on the earth today, each with his own particular angel to steer him in the right direction?

Guardian angels are so marvelous to have around. We know that no matter what awful things lie before us or how frightened we are, we are never, ever alone. Right now, right there beside you, your angel stands ready to protect you from any danger.

Our angels not only defend us from harm to our bodies but also to our souls. As the psalmist sings, "He has given his angels charge over thee to keep thee in all thy ways." They help us to pray, to fight back when we are tempted. They warn us when to steer clear of people or places which will turn us away from our Lord. And their final job, after a lifetime of watching over us, is to lead us safely into heaven.

Only when they present us to God at his throne can they rest

and enjoy heaven with us. We should be the best of friends, for no one outside of God and Mary will ever know us as well as our own angel.

Sometimes we may see our angel, if he wishes us to, but more often it is enough that we simply feel his presence. He may take any shape he chooses. He may be a policeman we've never seen before who comes to our aid when we are lost in traffic. Or a very nice old lady in the market (whom we've never seen before) who returns the $5 bill we dropped on the floor. Or the nurse in the hospital who brings a drink of water during the night and who never appears again.

I know a mother who stood on the shore of an angry ocean, screaming for help as she watched her two little children being pulled out to sea by the undertow. Suddenly, a man appeared out of nowhere, a stranger. He ran past her, plunged fully clothed into the roaring waves, and grabbed the children just as they were at the crest of a wave that would have taken them beyond reach. He brought them, one in each arm, to their mother, who hugged them as if she would never let them go. When she turned to thank the man, he was gone. Disappeared, never to be seen again. She knows he was *somebody's* guardian angel.

St. Frances of Rome had an angel who came to her in the form of an eight-year-old boy. He visited with her and they sat and talked about things and he wrote her notes in gold lettering in her prayer book. She describes him: "His aspect is full of sweetness and majesty. Words cannot describe the divine purity of his gaze!"

Other saints have loved these companion angels too. Augustine

taught that "the angels watch over us poor pilgrims. They have compassion on us and hasten to our aid at God's command. Go where
we will, they are always with us."

And Jerome believed that "so sublime is the dignity of the soul that
from its birth, there is appointed to each one a guardian spirit."

And Bernard told us to "Revere your guardian angel! Be grateful
for the care he bestows on you! Have confidence in him, love him,
and turn to him to entreat his protection in every difficulty, danger,
and temptation! Make the holy angels your friends!"

There is a family I know with lots of noisy, scrapping children
who are always getting bumped and falling down stairs and tripping
over dogs and shoelaces. Every morning when they dash out the
door for the school bus, their mother says a prayer to their guardian
angels so she won't worry about them during the day.

And at night, just before they go to bed, they say the same prayer
for themselves and for all their friends who live far away:

> O Angel of God,
> My guardian dear,
> To whom God's love
> Commits me here,
> Ever this night,
> Be at my side,
> To light, to guard,
> To rule and guide.

Then, as they lie down on cool pillows, they never for a moment have to worry about burglars or bats or spooks who tug at the blankets or wolves that scratch at the door or spiders that come down from the ceiling in the dark and land in their hair.

Guardian angels are *such* a comfort!

Francis of Assisi

October 4

Have you ever wondered who is the patron saint of moles and cockroaches and three-toed sloths and lizards that sleep under rocks? Is there anyone who watches over cabbage moths and shamrocks and woolly bears who inch across a busy road? Does anyone give a hoot about the rowdy screech owl?

Of course someone does, and his name is Francis of Assisi. He called himself God's fool, Brother Ass and *Il Poverello*, the little poor man. But we call him the saint for everyone and everything. He loved every bit of the world God had created and said we were all part of one family with one Father. Wind and sun, gnats and fishes, fire and ice—all were his sisters and brothers. Nor would he close the door on pain or death, for they too were relatives in this family.

Francis really began his life as John, but because his father, Pietro Bernardone, traveled often to France and his mother was French, they nicknamed him *Il Francesco*, the little Frenchman, and from that came *Francis*. Pietro was a wealthy cloth merchant in the town of Assisi, and from the time he could walk, Francis loved to toddle about the shop, touching the bolts of velvet and lace and satins which the noble ladies came to buy. He could not wait until he could wear fine clothes from these goods and look every inch the dashing rich boy he was.

Francis spent his youth without a worry or care to make him frown. Every day was an adventure, every night a party that never stopped, filled with wine and pastries and loud joking and singing till the sky grew light. Francis was small and quick and cheerful as a sparrow—but a sparrow dressed in the finest of red velvet, wearing gold rings and chains and silver buckles on his shoes.

Whatever mischief was planned by the young men of the town, you can be sure Francis was the ringleader. He didn't care about work or school, nor did he think long, heavy thoughts about life. He just played, or he dashed about on his horse over the Umbrian hills, exulting in the great fun of living. He drank too much and sang too much, and he danced till there were holes in the soles of his shoes. Pietro and Pica, his mother, just shook their heads and smiled.

"Boys will be boys," his father shrugged. "Why shouldn't he enjoy himself? He's only young once! And why should he worry about working? We've got all the money he needs."

And the townspeople shook their heads and smiled. Yes, Francis was a rascal, but such a warm, loving rascal, you couldn't get angry with him. And he was so generous—he never refused anyone a request. He would grow up and become a soldier or a knight and that would straighten him out.

By the time he was 20, he had his first chance to act as a knight for his country. Assisi was part of the province of Umbria, and Umbria and its neighbor, Perugia, were always at war over something. Anything could start it. It could be something as small as the smell from a Perugian pig farm that wafted over to Umbria and curdled the milk. Whatever the reason, a war broke out between the two provinces and Francis was the first to jump on his horse to fight for the honor of Umbria.

Before he had time to get hurt, the young soldier was captured, along with his friends, and spent a year in a Perugian prison. Even in such a depressing spot, he kept up everyone's spirits with his foolishness. He told jokes that were so silly people had to laugh even as they groaned. He sang old drinking songs, dancing around the cell with a make-believe violin of two sticks tucked under his chin. He made funny faces behind the jailers' backs. Nothing could keep him down, and he marked off the days on the wall till he could go back to the good times awaiting him at home.

Then the war ended as suddenly as it began and Francis burst out of the prison, free at last. He walked toward home happily, quickly, breathing in the good Umbrian air. He wondered if his clothes would still be in style. No matter, his father could have the best tailor zip him up a new tunic and trousers in no time. Suddenly he stopped, his way blocked by a man in ragged, smelly clothes. The man, who was a beggar, simply sat in the middle of the road with open hands.

He looked up at Francis with sadness in his eyes. Francis did not want to meet a beggar today. It was too depressing, but his heart was too tender to allow him to pass by.

"Please, sir, could you spare some money so I might buy a coat to keep warm? Not an expensive one, but a little, cheap, thin one to keep the chill off." He looked at Francis and sighed. "I used to have a red velvet cape like yours, once, long ago . . . when I was a knight."

Francis at once took off his clothes and tossed them to the shivering man. "Here, my friend, now give me yours so I can go home in style!" What a good joke it would be to arrive home like that! The beggar wanted to hug him but he didn't because he knew he was dirty and smelly. So Francis hugged *him*, and went on his way, whistling, to Assisi.

He went back to his old life, free to do and have everything he wanted. But something was wrong. All the old pleasures did not excite him. They seemed rather dull and childish now. He would leave parties to go out to look off into a sky full of stars, seeking he knew not what. His friends teased him. "What pretty girl are you dreaming of tonight, Francis?"

And one night he answered, very quietly, "A lovely one, more lovely and pure than I shall ever know again. Her name is Lady Poverty, and she shall be my bride."

This was certainly strange talk from someone who had never before been serious. His friends remembered that he had had a bout with a fever when he was in prison. Perhaps he hadn't recovered completely? But Francis was not feverish. He saw coolly and clearly the life ahead of him, and with all the joy he had given to his troubadour songs, he began his lifelong hymn to God.

One day when he was sitting in the Church of St. Damian wondering just how he would marry Lady Poverty, a voice coming from the crucifix on the wall said to him, "Francis, rebuild my house which is in ruins." Francis had no doubt that this was God telling him to repair the Church of St. Damian, which was old and crumbling and just about falling down.

So he went immediately to his father's store, took down several bolts of the finest satin, and sold them for a good deal of money. He ran with it to the pastor of St. Damian and gave it to him to repair the church, but the pastor didn't seem very happy about this great gift.

First of all, this young man was a bit strange. Where did he get so much money? Stole it most likely. The priest was just starting to say *no, thank you,* when the door burst open and there stood Francis' father, furious and with fists clenched. He grabbed Francis by the collar and shook him up and down. How dare he steal from his own father!

He dragged Francis home and locked him in his room until he would come to his senses and apologize. Pica, his gentle mother, came and begged him to do this so they could go back to being a happy family again. But Francis said he could not. "God told me to rebuild his church and I must obey him."

So his father brought him before the Bishop and the Church court to shame his son publicly. Pietro was hurting inside. All the high hopes he had for his son were dashed. His friends would think him a fool to be proud of such a one as Francis.

The Bishop listened to Pietro and then to Francis. Then the Bishop shook his head. "Francis, if you want to serve the Lord, you can't do it by stealing. You cannot use stolen money for the Lord; it has to be freely given."

Francis replied that from now on he would call only God his Father. He took off his fine silk blouse and velvet knickers, his dancing shoes and rings and chains and laid them at his father's feet. He stood naked in front of the Bishop and said now he owned nothing and owed nothing. The Bishop came down and wrapped his cloak around Francis' shoulders and embraced him. Pietro picked up the clothes and shoes and ornaments and walked away without a word. He no longer had a son.

Francis went off with a joy it is hard to describe. Now he was truly poor, like Christ, with absolutely nothing to his name but an old brown tunic that looked like a nightshirt, gathered in with a length of rope. He had no purse, no bread, no Bible, nothing but his absolute trust in God as a loving Father.

He was dancing a little jig down the road when a group of bandits saw him carrying on and decided to rob him. They thought he was probably drunk so they'd have an easy time taking whatever he had. They grabbed him and searched him up and down, then threw him into a ditch, disgusted because they found nothing. Francis was still singing.

"Keep quiet, you crazy loon," growled one of them, "or we'll give you something to howl about! Who are you anyway?"

Francis climbed up out of the ditch, rubbing away the blood from his scratches, and bowed low. "I am the herald of the King!" He laughed and continued his dance down the road.

He went back to St. Damian and, with the pastor's permission, he began to repair the old church by himself. He was as clever with his hands as he was with his mind, and the work he did with stone and wood and bricks was a pleasure to the eye.

One Sunday, when the work was done, he was listening to the Gospel and the words came into his heart and refused to budge:

"If you would be perfect, go and sell all you have and give it to the poor."

And, "Take nothing for your journey, neither purse nor bread, nor yet two coats nor staff."

And now he had an idea of what he was to do, what God had been trying to tell him. He was not to restore parish churches. He was to renew *the* Church.

So Francis went about preaching poverty and trust in God. It was very simple, so simple the people could not believe his message. He was called an impossible dunce, a vagabond, a leech who lived off other people. How dare he tell them that poverty was the one true way to Christ? Hadn't they been poor all their lives? And that love of God and one's neighbor was the only way to find peace? He was laughed at by people who were once his friends. His old neighbors scolded him for bringing such shame to his parents. And they threw rotten fruit and eggs and dead, disgusting things at him.

Francis wondered whether he had heard God right. Surely he would win no hearts here! But God answered him quickly. Before long a wealthy merchant, richer even than Francis' father, heard him preach and joined him. And then a priest, and then a woodcutter. Before long there were 12 of them, God's beggars, who went about preaching and begging for their food and sleeping on the ground or in caves at night.

One night Francis had a vision of hundreds of brothers in brown robes coming towards him and a voice saying to him, "I have chosen you to proclaim my Kingdom!" The next day, he went out and begged paper, ink and pen so he could set down the rules for his new order, which he would call the Friars Minor.

The Friars would, above all, trust in the Lord completely for all their needs. They would love all created things as their sisters and brothers. They would own nothing, not money, or land, or even a Bible. "If we own anything," Francis said, "we must have weapons to defend it, from which come quarrels and battles."

He rolled up his papers and took his Rule to Rome for the Pope's approval. The Pope was charmed by the little man with the dark, burning eyes, but he would not give his consent. He thought the Rule too strict, too hard. Why, sleeping on the ground like that, and not even owning a change of clothes! It was impossible to be that perfect.

But that night, *he* had a dream. He saw the great church of St. John Lateran falling, crumbling into dust, and only one ragged little man was holding it up. It was Francis. Our Lord said to the Pope, "This is the man through whom the Church shall be rebuilt."

The next morning the Pope called Francis to him and gave him his blessing. The Friars Minor were now officially approved. (They were called Minor so they wouldn't be tempted to be Major, or greater than anyone else.)

The order grew and grew, just as Francis had seen in his vision, and the brothers' influence on the people who listened to them was great. Soon the brothers went out of Italy; two by two they preached missions all over Europe. And everywhere they went, people listened.

And when Francis spoke, *all* his brothers and sisters hung on to his every word. The animals were as close to him as his human brothers. They sat quietly as he told them stories of our Lord's love for them and why they each had special colors or markings. He called the crested lark Brother Friar because he was dressed in a brown habit and hood. He told the robin that her breast was red because when she came to comfort our Lord on the cross, she pricked herself on his thorny crown.

And the frightened brown rabbit that nestled in his arms was comforted by his promise that her fur would turn white by the time the first snow fell, so she would be safe from foxes and hunters.

He had a way with larger animals too, especially a very large, angry, ferocious, ravenous wolf. This wolf had frightened the people in the town of Gubbio half to death. And those he didn't frighten to death, he ate. For some time, he made a habit of eating a person a day.

The terrified people thought he was a savage beast who ate them out of hatefulness. They never stopped to think that wolves get hungry, too. But the wolf and the people never got close enough to each other to try to talk things over.

When Francis came to Gubbio to see if he could talk to the wolf, the people had locked themselves in their homes. They peered out from behind curtains to watch this little man, who was brave but certainly not very bright.

Suddenly the hated wolf sprang out from behind a gooseberry bush. He was snarling and hissing and foaming at the mouth and had the wildest red eyes and yellow fangs Francis had ever seen. Just

as he was about to land on Francis and probably crush him, Francis called out, "Brother Wolf! Stop right this moment and hear God's Word!" And he quickly made the Sign of the Cross over the beast.

The wolf fell in a heap at the little man's feet and began whimpering. Francis saw that his ribs showed through his skin, like bars on a cage, and that the hair of his tail was scraggly and flat, as if it didn't have the strength to stand up even in anger.

"Brother Wolf," said Francis as sternly as possible (which wasn't very stern at all), "I command you, in our Lord's name, never to eat anyone again! Or do any harm to this town, ever. It's your town, too, you know. And you're not to knock over garbage pails or bite the heads off tulips when you feel out of sorts. Do you promise?"

The wolf hung his head and said nothing.

"Why have you done all these awful things?" asked Francis.

"I was hungry," sobbed the wolf. "All night long, I couldn't sleep because my stomach growled and kept me awake. Then I went out looking for food to keep my stomach quiet—nuts, berries, bark, *anything*—but there was nothing. One week all I had was an old shoe and a bunch of thistles, and thistles are very bad on your throat. Then I ate a little boy's hat and that wasn't bad, so I went back and ate the little boy. And then my stomach didn't growl."

So Francis told him how wrong this was, that no one could take the life of another, even if all he had to eat was thistles. He told him that God loved him and would see to it that he'd never be hungry again, and that the good people of Gubbio would feed him every day if he promised never to harm them.

So the wolf promised and gave Francis his paw to seal the promise.

And from that time on, the wolf was like a big pet dog. He even let the children ride on him.

Of all the creatures, the birds were Francis' pets. Whenever he preached, they would gather and crowd the trees and towers and chimneys. Larks and linnets and turtle doves and yellow-bellied sapsuckers and chickadees and sea gulls—they would twitter and chirp and warble and shriek, until their song drowned out Francis' words. Once they made such a racket Francis had to ask them please to be quiet.

"Sister birds, you have had your say, now please let me have mine. My word is from God and it is for you, too, to hear." So they quietly lowered their beaks, hid their heads in their wings, and not a whisper was heard until Francis was finished. And *then* were they loud!

On the evening Francis died, a gathering of larks swelled overhead and dipped and soared and sang their hearts out in their grief over losing him. Francis, who lay naked on his Sister Earth, smiled and whispered weakly, "My sweet sisters! No angel choir could pierce my heart as does your song. When I can no longer hear it, I know I shall be in heaven!"

And then they flew closer to one another and formed a cross of fluttering brown wings. They soared higher and higher, until the cross was but a pinprick in the heavens, and their song as faint as a child singing himself to sleep.

When the song of the larks could no longer be heard, the body of Francis lay still on the earth. His sisters had brought their brother home, and what excitement this caused in heaven.

You wouldn't believe that party! Honey and almond cakes

(Francis' favorite) and pistachio ice cream and cherry soda—enough for everyone in heaven. (Since people in heaven do not make pigs of themselves, there is always enough.)

Then a cricket hopped out of Francis' pocket and began to fiddle a dance. And Francis jumped up, all glowing and smiling as when he was a boy, and danced and sang and fiddled in his foolish joy—and this time he had a *real* violin.

Back on earth, the brown rabbit who would soon grow white and hide in the snow heard the commotion and twitched her whiskers with delight. She thumped out her message to those on earth and above and below:

"Francis is home, alive and well!"

Hedwig

October 16

ONCE UPON A TIME, there was a slip of a girl named Hedwig who was born into a royal family in Bavaria. Everyone exclaimed over the beauty of this child, whom God had fashioned as delicately as a china figurine. Her mother called her "my golden girl," and Hedwig was truly as warm and bright as a sudden shaft of sunlight shining through the window on a winter's afternoon.

She gave her parents no problems at all. She sat patiently as servants wove ribbons through her golden braids. She sipped her tea without ever making a noise. She was every inch the young countess of the castle and might have been that forever, had God not decided otherwise.

For six years she lived as the loved and loving child of Count Berthold and his wife, and then her parents took her to live at a nearby monastery in Kissingen. Here she would learn everything she would need to know as the future wife of a count or prince or whomever her parents would choose for her. She was taught to play the harp and embroider with pearls and paint flowers on china plates, and she could plan a banquet for a hundred princes and their wives without getting flustered. Here also she grew in her love for God. She wished in her heart that she might stay here forever, to love and serve him quietly and never go back to the world again.

But our Lord told Hedwig he had other plans for her. She waited patiently for him to explain, all the while she was sewing and lettering and learning to make tea from herbs. Then, when she was 12 years old, he did. Her father brought her the news that she was to be the wife of Prince Henry, the son of his good friend Boleslav the Tall of Silesia, which was in the far-off land of Poland.

Hedwig was shaken and sad, but she tried not to let her feelings show. (It wouldn't have done her any good even if she had, because in those days, marriages were arranged by parents, often before their children were born. Sometimes this was a sad situation. The brides and grooms, often very young, had no choice but to make the best of it. So for the glory of God, country and family, they married people they had never met and often didn't like when they did.)

But Henry and Hedwig felt their marriage was truly made in heaven (which, of course, it was). From the moment they met on their wedding day, they knew they would never love anyone else as they did each other. Even the sorrow of packing and leaving her family to live in a strange land was not as strong as Hedwig's desire to be the perfect wife for Henry.

As for the Prince, he soon discovered that his bride was as inquisitive as she was beautiful. She wanted to know everything about everything in her new home. She began asking questions from the moment she set foot in the royal carriage that would take them to Silesia. Why was there so much snow? Why were there so many prisons and no hospitals? How do you make beet soup? Why did the peasants never smile?

And when Henry replied it was because they were poor and hungry, Hedwig would ask *why* they were poor and hungry.

Henry smiled and answered that it was not for her to be concerned. She was his wife, a mere woman, and was not to think of unpleasant things. But he soon discovered that Hedwig had too quick a mind to forget what she saw. Her desire to know the *why* and *how* of everything made Henry look for the answers himself.

He began to ask her advice on all sorts of things, about taxes and gold mines and hunting bear and growing buckwheat. Hedwig always seemed to know how to solve a prickly problem. With a nod or touch or gentle questioning, she helped guide his heart to the right solution:

"Free these prisoners so they may see God's love through you!"

"Look at those little children shivering together. They must have wool coats and caps and mittens to keep warm, and boots lined with fur so their toes will not freeze!"

"My husband, the mothers need rye bread and sour cream and fresh eggs. Surely once a week you can share our bounty with them!"

Quietly, like drops of rain that will not cease, her desire to help her people wore through Henry's indifference. He began to see they had equal claim with him to God's love. Hedwig reminded him whenever he tired of doing good, "You know, Henry, but for the grace of God, *you* could be the thief in prison and I could be the mother with nothing to feed her babe. We are who we are for a reason."

And so, despite himself, Henry became a ruler who truly cared about his people. And he was the first to admit it was because of Hedwig. He loved his wife more than life itself and could not bear to say no to her requests, even if he didn't agree about their importance. When he would see a certain sweetly-determined look in her eye as they talked at breakfast, he would sigh and pretend to groan.

"Now what, my little Jadwiga! You want flannel underwear for all the servants because it is drafty in the castle? Such nonsense! It's good for them to be cold. It builds their character and keeps them humble. But all right, all right, they shall have it of course. Just don't look at me with those sad eyes."

By the time she was 26, Hedwig had six children. They were quarrelsome, and she had her hands full trying to teach them to love one another and not fight every moment of the day. Sometimes she thought they stopped only when they ate, and even then they would throw their mashed potatoes in a fit of temper.

Whenever she had a free moment away from the children, Hedwig continued to try to make life easier for her people. She felt that the time had come to build the country's first monastery school for women. Women who could not read or write were not a blessing to anyone, she told Henry. She wanted them to learn these things and then study astronomy and medicine and music. Then they could go and teach others as they had been taught.

Henry said, "Absolutely not!" The country could not afford such a luxury, women did not need to read or write, and that was that.

Hedwig gave the matter back to God. "Please, Lord," she prayed, "you put this idea into my head. Now please help me to make it come true."

The next day Henry decided they should all go hunting in the

great forest. It was the first time he had refused his wife anything and he wanted to make it up to her. So off they went, Henry and Hedwig and their servants, dressed in furs and scarlet robes.

Henry galloped ahead to clear a path—and he found himself on a road which was not known to him. The ancient oaks seemed to close in on him and the path became as narrow as a foot trail in the woods. Suddenly, the ground beneath Henry's horse became soft and the horse swiftly began to sink. No matter how he struggled, Henry could not pull the horse out of the mucky marsh. Up to his knees in mud, Henry realized in a flash that not all the gold in his treasury could save him now. What good was his money, his power!

He remembered his wife's pleading for a women's monastery and called out to God, "My Lord, help me get out of this, and upon my return, I shall build your women a marvelous, incredible monastery!"

And the horse sprung forward as if the angels had lifted him and cleared the mud. He carried the weary prince back to Hedwig, who already knew what had happened before Henry told her.

And so the monastery at Trebnitz was built with the help of all the prisoners Henry freed in exchange for their work. As the years passed, monasteries and hospitals popped up wherever there was need. It would seem that this would be enough to keep the royal couple busy, but this is just what they did when they were *relaxing*.

Most of their energy went into surviving wars. It was a time when wars were as expected as snow in winter. There were wars to keep out savage invaders, wars among the ruling princes of Poland, even wars between their own sons when they grew up and began fighting in earnest.

One enemy who constantly worried Henry was Swatopluk of Pomerania. Henry and Hedwig could not lay their heads down and rest easy, for they never knew when the wily leader would strike.

With great cunning, Swatopluk once chose the moment when Henry was helpless in his bath to rush in and slash him with his sword. This made Henry furious. Despite his bleeding wound, he jumped out and chased the scoundrel into the hills without even grabbing a towel. Henry escaped with his life—barely.

Hedwig brought herbs and ointment for his cut and brewed tea with lemon and whiskey to cure his shivers. But as soon as he took a few sips, he had to get dressed and be off to fight yet another enemy, Conrad of Plock, who was every bit as mean as Swatopluk.

With God's help, Henry defeated Conrad and set up his new kingdom at Krakow. While he was at Mass giving thanks, Conrad crept in and captured him, tied him up, and carried him off.

When Hedwig heard about this, she put on her gray cloak and followed her husband. With her gentle persuasion, she coaxed the two angry men to come to peace with each other.

"For shame," she said, "you are both Poles; why do you fight each other? And Conrad, I have good news for you. We would like your daughters to marry our sons! Now is this any way to give them a good start?" The men listened and agreed and from that time on treated each other as friendly relatives. Hedwig thanked the Lord that she had been able to stop a little killing for a little while.

The years passed and the children grew up and moved away. Hedwig and Henry realized they had grown old. Soon, they knew, their love story on earth would be over, but they were not sad. They knew the best was yet to come—a brand new life in heaven!

When Henry died, the nuns at the monastery of Trebnitz cried and cried. But Hedwig sat quietly with dry eyes and kept knitting mittens from odd bits of yarn. She comforted the nuns.

"Why are you crying, dear sisters? Our lives are God's. He puts us here for his own reasons and, when our work is done, we go on to do other work. When the bread is baked, we take it out of the oven, don't we? Come, let us rejoice. Dear Henry is stirring things up in heaven!"

Hedwig lived the rest of her life with the sisters at Trebnitz but did not become a nun. She kept the freedom of a royal princess so she could go out and continue to nurse the sick and work with the poor. Her son, Henry the Good, became king and continued to fight the invaders of Poland as his father had.

One day, as she used up the last bits of yarn in a pair of baby bootees, she called the sisters to her and said it was time for her to leave them and would they please call the priest.

They told her she was silly for she was in the best of health. "No," she said, "I want him *now*." So the priest came and when he touched her forehead with the oil, Hedwig smiled. "Look," she called out excitedly, "don't you see them? A whole procession of angels is coming in!"

And a great light shone about her head, as dazzling as a crown of diamonds catching the sun. Jadwiga, the little Lily of Poland, left with her heavenly escort to join her waiting husband. They met in a celebration that went on and on and on for *days*.

Hedwig said it was better than a Polish wedding.

All Saints' Day

November 1

Come out, come out
Wherever you are!
In bed or boat
Or under the car,
Planting a lily,
Braiding a rug,
Stirring up chili,
Dissecting a bug,
Milking a cow,
Stuffing a pillow,
Extolling a star,
Stripping a willow —
Come out, come out
From near and far!

For today is the day,
The first of November,
To celebrate saints
You may not remember.
The Big Ones you know,
They stand quite tall,
Like Francis and Vincent

And Peter and Paul,
But in their shadow
The unknowns cluster,
Loved by God
As a hot dog its mustard.

This is the day our Father has made
For Crispin and Nestor and sweet Adelaide,
And Wiltrudia and Finnian and Adalbert and Emma,
And Audrey and Priscilla and Paphnutius and Otto,
And Zachary and Flora and Isaac of Cordova,
And Winifred and Poppo and Blessed Rizzerio.

This is the day the King has given
To Meinrad and Thecla and Bruno and Swithin,
To Olaf of Norway,
And Eric of Sweden,
Mechtilde of Hackeborn,
And Simeon, Armenian,
To Trumwin and Jutta and Hilda and Chad,
And Dymphna and Botwid and Ethelnoth and Gall,
To Gerlac and Munchin, Nutburga and Narcissus,
Who served him on earth, who gave him their all.

This is the day our Lord decrees
Diadem and doves and gifts that will please
To Ptolemy and Englebert, Modwenna and Canute,

And Ida of Toggenberg and Gertrudia of Delft,
And Blessed Thomas Plumtree and Josephat of Plotsk,
And Oswald of Northumbria and little John the Dwarf.

    Come out, come out,
    And stand in the sun!
    For this is the day for all holy ones,

For saints true-tested and those not done
Who live right now, daughters and sons:

The man with warts who trims your tree,
The librarian who stamps your books,
And Alice Gray, who sings sad songs,
And the lady in school who cooks,

The teacher who gives you too much homework,
The priest who is fat and sweaty,
Your cousin who always does everything better,
The clown who throws confetti.

Come out, come out,
Bake cakes or trout!
Come, sit down and rest awhile,
Adjust your crown and royal smile,
Curl your hair, make a fuss —
This is the day for *all* of us!

Martin de Porres

November 3

Once upon a time, there was a saint who could fly through the air faster than a bird, a passing bullet, or the speed of light. He wasn't Superman or even Supersaint. He was Martin de Porres.

Martin wasn't a saint because he could fly, and he didn't fly because he was a saint. Flying, or *teleporting*, was only one of the incredible gifts which God had given him. These were spectacular, eye-popping, now-watch-this-one gifts, like fireworks that bring forth ooooh's and aaaah's as they burst upon the sky.

Our Lord, with his divine sense of humor, chose someone you'd least expect to perform his magic, a sweet, humble man who would have been just as happy sweeping floors or saving mice. His name was Martin de Porres and he was born in Lima, Peru, in the 16th century. Like Rose of Lima, who lived at the same time and was his friend, he knew from childhood that all he wanted to do with his life was give it to the Lord.

And, like Rose, he was the son of a Spanish aristocrat. Unlike Rose, he was a *mulatto*, which means that one of his parents was white and the other black. Their way of life was different from birth. Yet, through their love for a God who knew no differences, Martin and Rose were drawn together as friends.

Martin was the natural son (which means his parents were not married) of Juan de Porres, a Spanish knight, and Anna, a black woman who had come to Peru from Panama. After Martin's sister Juana was born, his father went away and left Anna to take care of herself and the children as best she could.

It was a struggle to make ends meet. Anna took in wash and Martin and Juana, little as they were, helped her scrub the bags of dirty laundry left by the Spaniards. The children had a sweet and sunny outlook, with no trace of resentment against those who had more than they (which was practically everyone). Martin was at times too generous, as far as his mother was concerned. He would exasperate her by giving away the money she gave him to buy food at the market or, if he got as far as the market to buy it, by giving the food away to beggars. He could not resist a tearful eye or quivering lip. Even chickens followed him home, knowing they would get the last of the corn or crumbs.

When Martin was 12, his father sent money to Anna to give the children an education. She apprenticed Martin to a barber because he had already shown a gift for healing. In those days, a barber was also a surgeon who sewed up cuts, set bones, cured fevers and applied poultices to wounds to draw out infections. So if you fell out of a tree and broke your arm the day you needed a haircut, you could take care of both at the same shop.

Martin loved this work. He woke each morning with excitement, wondering what good he would do with his hands and skill that day. He was satisfied that he would spend his life curing all those who came to him. This would be his work for God.

But God told Martin he wanted more. One night, as he lay weary and happy on his cot in the barbershop, God woke him.

"Martin," he whispered, "I want you to use your gifts for helping others, but first I want you to serve me with prayer and penance."

Martin understood. And his mother and sister understood. He said good-bye to them (but not forever since they would still be in the same town) and went off to the Dominican monastery of the Holy Rosary. Here he knew his life would be centered around God from dawn to dark. He asked the monks if he might join them, not as a priest or a brother, but as a servant of all of them. He wanted to be a *donado*, one who gives himself completely to God in the service of others.

The Prior was delighted to accept this young boy (he was just 15) whose healing skill was already well-known to him. Martin's father, Juan, who had come back to Lima on a visit, was quite annoyed. Even though he didn't actually want to *be* Martin's father—after all, the boy had skin the color of coffee with cream—he expected the boy to remember his noble origin.

"The least you could do," he sniffed, "is become a priest, not a servant."

But Martin knew what he was doing. He didn't want the comfort or high esteem of being a priest. He wanted to take on the lowliest tasks, and he did. He swept and scoured and made beds and cleaned out garbage pails and stables. He washed the altar linens and the brothers' habits. He gathered herbs and flowers for ointments and teas. In short, he did anything he was asked.

Lima had been taken over by Spanish conquerors such as Martin's father. Even though they had killed the natives and had stolen their land and gold, they considered themselves good Christians.

They did not see themselves as they really were—cruel, selfish and un-Christlike. Instead, they painted pictures of themselves inside their minds as generous men of God. So to balance the evil they did, they gave huge amounts of money to be used for the poor.

And his superiors asked Martin to take care of seeing that everyone got a fair share. It was hard to find an honest man in those days, but Martin had become known as a completely honest person in handling money, one who would never keep anything for himself. Because he always said yes, Martin was quick to put his broom away and go forth to work with the poor, whom he had always loved.

Every week he used every bit of $2,000 for food and medicine and clothing. He gave it to poor boys who wished to become priests and to poor girls who wanted to marry or enter a convent. He used it to found an orphanage and to free prisoners. And if he had any pennies left over, he bought very ripe bananas so the baker at the monastery could make a treat of banana bread.

While he was taking care of the poor outside the monastery, he was still taking care of the aches and pains of the monks within. Because he could heal so quickly and naturally, the word spread into the town about the wonder-worker who cured with a touch of his hand. Each day, more and more people waited at the door of the infirmary, clamoring to see Martin. It began to look like a large city clinic, with long lines of people coming and going all day long.

The monks began to complain. It wasn't healthy having all these sick people coming to the monastery, they said. So Martin's sister Juana, who had a home of her own by now, opened her doors to them. She must have been as generous and loving as her brother.

We know very little about her, but I wouldn't doubt that she is a saint, too.

Martin's gift of healing gave much glory to God but it also gave Martin a headache. He had chosen to live the hidden life of a *donado*, trying to be the least among men. Yet he had been given these extraordinary gifts. He didn't ask for them and maybe he really didn't want them—but he had them! There was no way out but to use them and to hold nothing back.

He used his natural skill and learning first and gave them the credit for his cures. But in his heart he knew that it was often just his touch that did it. In such cases, he would make a joke of it or give some simple remedy as the cure, treating it lightly.

Once he treated the Governor of Mexico for a very sore throat with a high fever. He was cured immediately by drinking the medicine which Martin had given him. It was just plain water! And another time, when a woman who was at death's door was healed, Martin said it was because she had eaten an apple as he had told her. (Maybe that's how we got the saying, "An apple a day keeps the doctor away." Well, it *could* be.)

Most of his cures occurred right within the monastery. Once there was a monk who had a fever for so long, it depressed him. The corner of his mouth turned down and he rolled his eyes and wore a long face which seemed to go on forever.

"I shall never get well," he moaned to Martin.

"Now, Brother," smiled Martin gently, "if you keep on saying that, you won't let yourself." Martin believed that being hopeful and

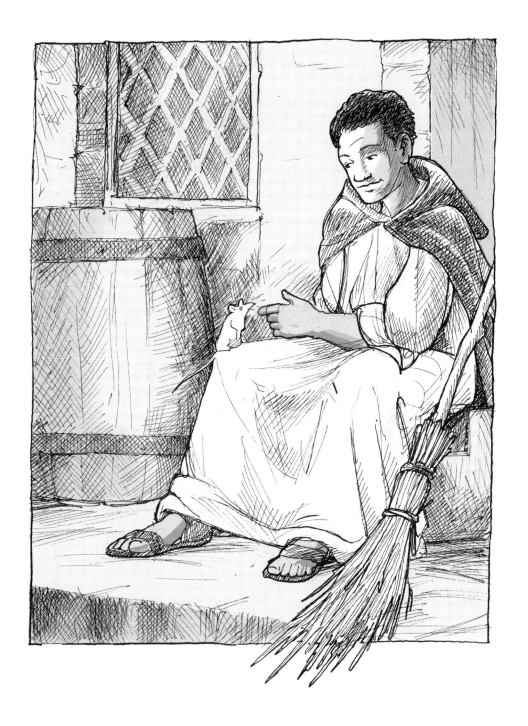

of good cheer was the best part of a remedy, so he tried to coax people out of feeling sorry for themselves.

He told the monk to take a bath in the monastery pond when night fell and he would feel much better.

"Is that all?" asked the monk, a bit disappointed at such simple medicine.

"That will do it," said Martin.

So the monk shrugged his shoulders and made his way to the pond that night. It was a very strange cure, he thought, but since he was probably going to die anyway, he'd try it.

He jumped into the pool but the water was so cold, he lost his breath and jumped back onto the grass. Then he was so cold he jumped back in. This time he stayed in so long he almost froze and got so numb he couldn't climb out. A brother happened to pass by and pulled him out and wrapped him in warm blankets. He fell asleep immediately and when he woke the next morning, he found he wasn't dead. As a matter of fact, he felt marvelous and ready for a huge breakfast. He was never sick again!

Martin's compassion for the animals who were part of God's family was as great as that for humans. He felt especially concerned for rats and mice because, he said, the poor little things weren't as lovable as cats and dogs. And he couldn't convince his brother monks not to set traps for them.

"They are nothing but pests, Brother Martin, vermin!"

To make matters worse, the mice had invaded the vestry and were making lacework of the vestments with their sharp teeth. One angry monk exploded, "How would you like to say Mass with your cassock full of holes?"

Martin could understand their impatience but still he could not bear to kill or even scold his scurrying, squeaking friends.

He came to them that evening as they were busily shredding the edges of a surplice. "My little brothers," he said gently, "you had better stop this mischief or you shall find yourselves caught in a trap and that will be the end of it. I can't protect you forever. Now, all of you, listen to me. Leave the monastery and go out to the garden, and I promise I will bring you food every day. It should be more enjoyable than this piece of cloth. Go, right now!"

And they did, every single one of them, as fast as you could blink an eye. They never again touched anything belonging to the church, and to the end of his days, Martin fed his mice in the garden.

It wasn't just mice who were charmed by his love. All animals obeyed him instantly. If you've ever tried to train your dog not to sleep on the couch, you know that it takes much patience and time to get animals to do what you want. But Martin had a special way with them. Chickens danced about his feet, mules and dogs and cats rubbed against him and thrust their heads into his hands so he could scratch behind their ears. He coaxed a mouse to eat from the same bowl as a cat and dog, and from that time on, they were all the best of friends.

The hospital at his sister's house soon included animal patients and a shelter for dogs and cats waiting to find homes. (Now I am sure Juana was a saint!)

One of the many stories about Martin and his animal friends is about a very old dog who belonged to the monk in charge of the kitchen at the monastery. This dog was very ancient—at least 18 years old—very slow, very clumsy with age. He had just about everything wrong with him, including a bad case of mange. He scratched and snuffled and wheezed and limped and, worst of all, he smelled. He smelled so bad the monks held their noses when he shuffled by, as if they had just smelled a skunk.

His owner decided sadly that he could no longer ask his brothers to put up with this, so he ordered the dog to be killed. While the dog stretched out in the sunshine, enjoying a nap, a servant threw a huge rock at the dog's head and killed him instantly. He was about to pick up the dog to throw him into the river when Martin stopped him.

He took the poor mangy, smelly animal into his arms and carried him into his room. No sooner did the dog touch the floor than he pulled himself up, put his nose into Martin's hand, and tried to move his head back and forth. Martin cleaned the wound and sewed up the skin and then poured wine over it. The dog became dizzy from it and lay down and slept.

The next morning Martin brought him a bit of meat, and he sniffed at it, then gulped it down. He wagged his tail, slipped through Martin's legs and ran off, completely cured—of *everything*. He smelled as clean as wash blowing dry in the wind. And he never again had to fear for his life.

All of these gifts would be enough to spread over a dozen saints, but Martin had even more startling ones. For one thing, he had the ability to rise in the air and stay there. He would sometimes become so rapt in his love for our Lord, the love would take over his body and make it light as a feather and bright as the sun. While at prayers he would often soar to the ceiling in the chapel or in his room. Once when a young novice was sent to find Brother Martin, he saw a brilliant light coming out from under the door to his room. He opened the door cautiously. Martin, who had risen off the floor, caught his foot in the novice's hood and nearly scared him out of his habit. It took quite a while for Martin to calm him down and help him realize this was nothing out of the ordinary.

For another thing, Martin could read minds. He often did this while cutting the hair of his brother monks. He would tell them gently that he knew what was troubling them (even if they always smiled and never admitted they were troubled) and give them the exactly right advice they needed. He could foretell the future. He knew who would leave the monastery and who would get up in the night and take food from the kitchen and who would sleep while they were supposed to be praying. He could even track down missing letters or people.

Once two novices disappeared. While he was praying, Martin read their minds (even though they were in another town). He whisked himself off and appeared to them through their locked doors. Once their fright wore off, he talked with them and told them that they really were meant to be monks; they were just tired and unsure right now. He put his arm around them and, in the wink of an eye, they were back at the monastery without anyone else ever knowing of it.

He had the gift of entering and leaving locked doors or barred windows without being seen. He walked through walls. Whenever he was needed, he was there, as if he had some special antenna that signaled an emergency. This ability led into an even more incredible gift—the gift of bilocation, which means that he could be in two places at one time. Now this sounds impossible. You know it's impossible because even your mother says, when three of you are yelling for her at once, "Will you please wait a minute, I can't be in two places at one time!"

But Martin could. While people saw him busy at work in Lima, he was traveling all over the globe, learning about new medicines in France, soothing the wounds of black slaves in Algeria, helping persecuted Christians in China and Japan. Wherever he was needed, he appeared.

You may think what fun you'd have if you had such powers! Why, you could eat hot dogs at a ball game in Baltimore or have the best seat in the house to see *The Nutcracker* ballet in New York. Or you could land in an ice cream factory and sample every single flavor until you got sick. And if you were sent to your room to study, you could always just fly out of the window and go to watch the changing of the guard at Buckingham Palace. The things you could do!

But Martin didn't do that. Whatever powers God gave Martin—the gifts of healing or reading minds or telling the future or raising the dead or flying through space—they were used only to bring glory to God. He did this so well he could be the patron saint of just about everyone. Barbers and beggars and pilots and locksmiths and magicians and nurses and veterinarians and old dogs and people with rats in their cellars and squirrels in their attics. He was like a jewel in the sun, giving off brilliance no matter how the rays caught it.

Yet whenever you see a picture of Martin, he is not doing anything as spectacular as flying through the air or walking through walls. You will see him with a broom in his hands and a mouse or two playing about his feet. This is the truest and most important picture, for it shows him as all he ever wanted to be—God's *donado*.

Now that he's in heaven, I wonder if Martin ever makes flying trips to earth when he's especially needed. Has any of you ever seen him?

Well, if ever I see someone in a black and white habit zooming across the sky, *I* won't be surprised. I'll know it's not an unidentified flying object. It's just Martin answering a call.

Frances Xavier Cabrini

November 13

Once upon a time, not very long ago, there lived a little girl named Mary Francesca who wanted to be a missionary to China more than anything else in the world. She would sit by a stream near her home and make boats out of empty pea pods. Then she would fill them with violets and pretend they were priests and nuns setting off on the journey to the East. Someday, she said, *she* would be doing that for real!

Mary Francesca, or Frances, was the 13th child born to a farming family in Lodi, Italy. You might think that the baby in such a large family would be terribly spoiled and determined to have her own way, but Frances was neither. Her sisters were quite strict and made her mind. (Anyone with many big brothers and sisters knows it is very hard to be spoiled with *them* around.)

At night, the family would read aloud from a book about the lives of the missionaries, and Frances thought again that this was exactly what she wanted to be. She practiced giving up candy and apricot pastries because she knew there would be nothing of that sort in China, so she had better get used to it. She wondered if she would have to eat raw fish when she got to China and prayed that if she did, God would give her the courage to swallow it quickly.

The years passed and young Frances grew up and became a

teacher. She enjoyed this work but didn't feel it was enough to satisfy all she wanted to do. Only working for God would do that.

Frances felt it was time to announce that she wanted to become a nun, and a missionary at that. She went to the Bishop and asked him if she might become a missionary and go to China.

"You want to join a missionary order?" he asked, with a slight frown. "Very well. I don't know of any, so go found one yourself."

Frances, who was very determined, set about doing just that. She, and seven young women as filled with grace and enthusiasm as she was, formed a society called the Missionary Sisters of the Sacred Heart. It wasn't a great success at first. Many people felt it just wasn't right for young women to be missionaries and to go off into strange lands. Frances would remind them that there is neither male nor female in the Lord and that all are equal in his sight.

Her good works in Italy soon won them over. Within a few years the sisters had set up schools for girls, homes for orphans, hotels for college students. Soon she opened two houses in Rome—a free school and a children's home.

One particular Bishop had been watching her and asked her to come see him. She did, wondering what was on his mind.

"Sister Frances," he began, "I have had my eye on you. I have in mind a missionary work of great importance for only the bravest, most determined believer in miracles. I believe you are the person God has in mind for me to send overseas!"

Frances was so excited her head spun. China, at last! She would sail to the Far East, not in a pea pod boat but in a real one.

"Frances," the Bishop said, "I want you to go to a foreign land—the United States, to work among our Italian people in New York City."

"Oh, no, thank you!" said Frances. She knew God wanted her to go to China, *not* New York City.

"But," he continued, "our people need you. They have so few priests to help them. They left here to find a new and better life for themselves. They thought they would never be poor or hungry again. Now, what do they find? They are ignored, pushed around, made fun of; they work in sweatshops and dirty streets. They are still poor and hungry, and they are losing their faith besides."

"No, thank you," she repeated, feeling a bit guilty.

The next day she received a letter from the Archbishop of New York, asking her please to come. And that night she had a dream in which the Pope came to her and said, "Not to the East, Frances, but to the West."

There was no question now. Frances went to the Bishop and said yes. Once she made up her mind to something, she went full steam ahead. She packed her bags and gathered six of her strongest (in body and spirit) sisters and together they set off on their voyage west.

When they arrived in New York City, they found no one to meet them and no place to go. They stopped at the nearest hotel, which looked very down-at-the-heels with cracked shades and missing window panes. All of them stayed in one room. It was so dirty, they didn't want to turn on the light.

When they did, they heard the scurrying of hundreds of cockroaches disappearing into the woodwork. Rats—or maybe very big mice—hurried softly and quickly up and down the inside walls. The sisters did not want to pull down the bedsheets for fear of what they might find, so they spent the night kneeling and praying for courage to meet whatever tomorrow would bring.

The next day the Archbishop came to them and said he was sorry but the plans had been changed. There was no longer a building for them, so perhaps they had better go back to Italy.

Frances answered before his words died on the air. "The Pope sent me here and here I stay." He was taken aback by this spunky little woman who seemed to fear no one and who believed that nothing was impossible.

The sisters went to work. First, after finding a small home for themselves where their people lived in a part of New York called Little Italy, they learned the English language. They found a nearby building which they used to take in orphans or whatever children needed a home. When they needed money, they went out to beg. They went from door to door and shop to shop, and even to the police stations. They would take anything—food, clothing, money— and it was always just what they needed at the moment.

Frances taught her sisters that the poor did not depend on their small works but rather upon God's working through them. She told them to "pray always and ask without ceasing, that is, have your mind always fixed on prayer, and will only what God wills." And, she urged, "Have faith and you will behold miracles!"

She proved those words in her life. She traveled up and down this country, from Chicago to New Orleans, from Scranton to

Denver, starting hospitals and schools and homes. She went to Central America and crossed the Andes Mountains on a mule. She crossed the ocean 30 times altogether to spread her work throughout England, France, Spain—and, yes, Italy.

When she was 59 years old, she became a citizen of the United States. She loved this land which had become her second home and which she now knew almost better than people born here. Many of you of Italian descent may have had grandparents or great-grand-parents who remember the little nun who brought comfort and the strength to keep going to her people all over this country.

She is our first American saint and is buried under the altar of Mother Cabrini High School in New York City.

Mary Francesca did not fulfill her childhood dream of sailing off to China to win souls. But neither did her patron saint, Francis Xavier, who died within sight of its shore.

God had other plans for them. So they discarded theirs and followed his, and that's all any of us have to do to become saints.